FUTHARK
RUNE MYSTERIES

"With this work, Judith Dillon brings us on a fascinating journey through the history of the Norse runes. The mystery and sacredness of this ancient written language are combined with linguistic and ethnographic science to render a fascinating account of the symbols' origins, evolution, and uses. Treating runic marks as paradigmatic examples of what Descartes called 'signs,' Dillon establishes the runes as the bones of a primal alphabet and symbolic system, locating the signs and their meanings securely within the Cartesian context of 'magically' productive, generative language—symbol systems that generate other varieties of thoughts, such as music and mathematics, art, and mystical divination."

Yvonne Owens, Ph.D., past research fellow at the University College of London, professor emerita of art history and critical studies, and coauthor of *The Witch's Book of Days*

FUTHARK
RUNE MYSTERIES

Origins of Magic and Divination in the Primal Alphabet

A Sacred Planet Book

JUDITH DILLON

Destiny Books
Rochester, Vermont

Destiny Books
One Park Street
Rochester, Vermont 05767
www.DestinyBooks.com

Destiny Books is a division of Inner Traditions International

Sacred Planet Books are curated by Richard Grossinger, Inner Traditions editorial board member and cofounder and former publisher of North Atlantic Books. The Sacred Planet collection, published under the umbrella of the Inner Traditions family of imprints, includes works on the themes of consciousness, cosmology, alternative medicine, dreams, climate, permaculture, alchemy, shamanic studies, oracles, astrology, crystals, hyperobjects, locutions, and subtle bodies.

Cataloging-in-Publication Data for this title is available from the Library of Congress

ISBN 979-8-88850-263-1 (print)
ISBN 979-8-88850-264-8 (ebook)

Printed and bound in the United States by Lake Book Manufacturing, LLC

10 9 8 7 6 5 4 3 2 1

Text design by Kenleigh Manseau and layout by Debbie Glogover
This book was typeset in Garamond Premier Pro with Arno Pro, Connemara Old Style and Gill Sans MT Pro used as display typefaces

To send correspondence to the author of this book, mail a first-class letter to the author c/o Inner Traditions, One Park Street, Rochester, VT 05767, and we will forward the communication.

Contents

3 ᚦ 43

Thurs: *Giant or Thorn*

4 ᚨ 50

Ansus: *High God*

Oss: *Mouth*

5 ᚱ 54

Raido: *Journey*

6 ᚲ 60

Ken: *Torch*

Kaun: *Ulcer*

7 ᚷ 66

Gyfu: *Gift*

8 ᚹ 73

Wunjo: *Joy*

Wynn: *White*

SECOND AETTIR

Hel's Family

9 ᚺ 83

Hagalaz: *Hail or Heal*

10 ᚾ 91

Naudiz: *Need*

11 ᛁ 97

Isaz: *Ice*

THIRD AETTIR
Tir's Family

Acknowledgments

I thank my family, including my sister Patricia, for their support over the years of my researching and writing this book. They listened patiently while I tried to explain my developing thoughts. I would like to give special thanks to Sue, who always knew it was the Cow. As always, thanks to Richard Grossinger, who was generous in including me in his lineage of authors, and editor Dorona Zierler and publicist Manzanita Carpenter for their suggestions. I would also like to thank the U.S. Games Systems, Inc. founder, Stuart Kaplan, for his extensive research on Tarot cards, which helped me unravel the ancient pattern underlying runes.

INTRODUCTION

The Magic of Runes

A Brief History of the First Alphabet

Once, there was no alphabet; then there was. The world's first alphabet emerged out of the magic of Africa and the mysteries of Egypt. It contained hints of star-watching Mesopotamians and a whiff of ancient Anatolia where feathered maidens once carried the dead toward lights in the sky. In time, Mysteries, hidden in this early alphabet, evolved into secrets of northern rune magic.

Long ago we knew a song to enchant a new world out of the dark. The hope for a return into the light of day is as old as our ancestors. Our dead were once buried in jars shaped like eggs and placed in tombs with faces looking toward the rising sun, cozily joining relatives under the floors of their homes or placed to watch the setting sun. They lay hoping to travel through the dark toward the light, waiting until their souls might shine again.

Thousands of years ago, there was a great melting pot of cultures spanning from the Black Sea by Anatolia, down to Mesopotamia, east toward India, across seas of grass toward China, and west toward Africa and the island of Crete. Traders and travelers wandered along high country passes and over sandy deserts or sailed increasingly sophisticated boats along the coasts of Canaan and out across the Green Sea.

Along with trade goods, they passed along secrets of time, magic, and measurements. Some of these secrets were couched in the symbols that became our first alphabet letters. Adapted by numerous peoples, these letter-symbols provided a common way to write among those speaking multiple unrelated languages. They also encoded a path promising a return to the light.

By 3000 BCE, Egypt had trade routes extending from Mesopotamia through the coastal cities of the Levant, the area eventually known as Canaan, and across the sea to Crete.

Canaan contained the rich coastal cities of an early Semitic people, including Tyre, Sidon, and Byblos. In their own language, their name was Kn'n, which claimed their descent from the biblical Cain. The first son of Adam and Eve, Cain possessed a mark protecting him from death. His descendants were credited with the skills of music, metalworking, and city building. While genetically and culturally related to other early Canaanites, the seafaring culture of their coastal cities quickly became distinct from other closely related tribes including the early Israelites.

By convention, these people were called Canaanites until around 1200 BCE, when the Greeks renamed them Phoenicians. The Canaanites/Phoenicians, like later Northmen, were both traders and pirates of the Mediterranean Sea. Wide-ranging sailors, they were part of an extensive trade between Egypt, the labyrinths of Crete, Greece, Anatolia, and the Near East.

Around 1800 BCE, an unknown person or persons took a handful of Egyptian hieroglyphs from among the thousands and adapted them to the West Semitic language spoken by the Canaanites/Phoenicians. Our first true alphabet is thought to be derived from hieroglyphic pictures which were renamed in the Semitic language.

The oldest examples of these letters were found in Canaan, near the Egyptian trade city of Thebes, and by the copper-turquoise mines of Sinai: areas frequented by the Western Semites. In addition to being traders, merchants, slaves, and skilled workers, they came as migrants fleeing drought to seek the green land of Egypt. Although modern scholars don't know who invented the alphabet, the Phoenicians are credited with its dispersal:

> The Egyptians [. . .] claim to have invented the alphabet, which the Phoenicians, they say, by means of their superior seamanship, introduced into Greece, and of which they appropriated the glory, giving out that they had discovered what they had really been taught. Tradition indeed says that Cadmus, visiting Greece in a Phoenician fleet, was the teacher of this art to its yet barbarous tribes.[1]

Mythology claims that the Phoenician Cadmus stole the alphabet from his ancestor, a great cow goddess. Some of the earliest letters were found in the temple of the cow goddess, variously known as Hathor, Isis, Io, and Balaat, near the copper and turquoise mines in the Sinai. This cow goddess was considered the protector of metalworkers, sailors, and seamanship, so her protection was important to the seafaring, metal-working Phoenicians. Another of the cow goddess's great temples, where both Egyptians and Semites worshipped, was in Byblos in Canaanite Phoenicia. This city of writing gives us such words as *bibliotheca* (library) and *bibliography*.

Regardless of who was the actual inventor, Egyptian scribes would not have used such a simple alphabet as their great income and prestige came from years of training to write hieroglyphs. After the early letters appeared circa 1800 BCE, they languished until they were transmitted around the ancient world by the Phoenicians, circa 1050 BCE.

In time, these early Semitic letters became the twenty-two letters that are the ancestors of all true alphabets. The earliest letters were not placed in a settled order until around 1300 BCE when they appeared in their present order in the Canaanite city of Ugarit.[2] By 1050 BCE, the letters became the alphabet known as Phoenician and its close cousin, Old Hebrew.

In this alphabet, each letter names an object and supplies a single sound. For instance, the first two symbols are Aleph, meaning "ox," with the sound of *a*, and Beth, meaning "house," with the sound of *b* (see "Symbols and Meanings of the Ancient Scripts," page 9). Although the Hebrew version kept the names and order of the early Phoenician symbols, the pattern of the letters was widely adapted by numerous peoples. In addition to providing the technology of writing, the order of the symbols hides alchemical secrets. That is, the attributes of each object chosen to represent the letters tell an evolving story of a passage through the dark into the light of another day. Each symbol represents a chapter in the secrets taught to a few initiates, possibly transmitted through trade guilds.

Associated with both writing and secretive mystery traditions, the Semitic alphabet from Egypt eventually supplied the mythic pattern, the "spells," underlying Germanic runes. As a caveat to scholars of ancient alphabets, I have no interest in describing how the original alphabet physically morphed into all the alphabets of the ancient world. My interest is in why the symbols chosen to represent the letters were placed in a specific order, with each position being associated with stories describing an evolving path through life and the afterlife.

When the Phoenicians transmitted the alphabet letters along with trade goods, they also transmitted the Mysteries of resurrection—the return from the dark—with which the letters are closely associated.* Like their ancestor Cain, the alphabet included a mark (Tau, the twenty-second letter) promising that death would pass them by. Their alphabet and its associated mystery traditions were adapted by the Greeks. As mentioned earlier, they had renamed the Canaanites, Phoenicians, a word derived from *phoenix*, which hints at these secrets. The phoenix, which appears in both Egyptian and Greek mythology, is a glowing firebird that rises, eternally reborn, from the blackened ashes of its destruction.

In Egypt, this resurrecting phoenix is associated with the palm tree, *phoenix dactylifera*, which bears the dates (dactyls) of each new calendar year. As a symbol representing the returning year, the palm tree is said to produce a new branch each month—twelve over the year. In Egypt, the phoenix, known as the Benu bird, returns after each Deluge to enchant a new world into existence. Benu is also the name for the palm tree midwifing Egypt's sun each new morning.†

---

*The Greek word *mysterion* implies both of a secret rite and initiation into these secrets.

†The word *Benu* in Egyptian means both "purple heron" and "palm tree." *Phoenix* also translates as "purple," the color of Phoenician dye.

Egypt, a country obsessed with light after each passage through the dark, was surely the source of the Mysteries encoded among the alphabet symbols:

> [Egyptians were] the first to broach the opinion that the soul of man is immortal, and that, when the body dies, it enters into the form of an animal which is born at the moment, thence passing on from one animal into another, until it has circled through the forms of all the creatures which tenant the earth, the water, and the air, after which it enters again into a human frame and is born anew. [Greek writers borrowing from Egypt] put it forward as their own.[3]

The palm represented eternal life, her fingers (dactyls) returning souls through childbirth. Later we will explore the use of birth runes (*bjargrúnar*) inscribed on the midwife's palms. In Greece, the palm midwifed the moon (Artemis) followed by her sun (Apollo): "The [palmtree] played midwife [to] Apollo and Artemis."[4] Among later Jews, the palm (Tamar) gave birth to the line of Judah, with the firstborn (Peretz) bursting forth like the moon.

Just as the seasons of a revolving year, the dates of the calendar, and the stars traveling the revolving sky always appear in a set order, so do alphabet letters. Order will prove important in understanding why each specific symbol was chosen as a letter. Each letter represented an object, and the first sound of the word for that object (e.g., the first sound of Aleph/ox is *a*), can write any number of words. In addition to representing sounds, an object can function as a mnemonic for a proper spell. A properly spelled word demands its letters in order.

Each letter-object of the Phoenician/Old Hebrew alphabet was determined by its numbered place in the order. The numbers are the key to finding our way through the labyrinth of alphabet myths. Numbers have roots in the lunar-solar cycles of the sky, and it is well accepted that ancient myths used the sky to illustrate their tales. Among later Jews, religious texts (Torah) are carefully transcribed. Not a single symbol can be changed or reordered without the mis-spell invalidating the Torah scroll.

As discussed earlier a Phoenician, the shining Cadmus, carried the alphabet and its hidden Mysteries to Greece. He had traveled there to look for his sister Europa, who had been kidnapped by Zeus in the form of a bull and carried to Crete.*

Early Crete had a script known as Linear A, which has not been translated. Before adopting the simple Phoenician shapes, Mycenaean Greeks† adapted the Cretan symbols to write Greek in Linear B. The Mycenaean civilization declined and was eventually destroyed between the eleventh and ninth centuries BCE, and the Phoenician alphabet replaced Linear B circa 1200 BCE.[5]

THRACE AND THE NORSEMEN

The kingdom of Thrace (also known as Thrudheim),[6] is named after the goddess Thrace, sister of Europa. Thrace, claimed by the Norse god Thor as his homeland, was located on the western side of the Black Sea. Although Odin, Thor's father, learned the secrets of runes near the Black Sea, he did not learn a builder's trade. He hired a giant Cyclops to build a palace fort there from huge stones using a technique known as Cyclopean masonry.

A fortress bearing a similar description was discovered in Bulgaria, which is on the border of Greece and is thought to prove that Thrace was a part of the Mycenaean civilization:

> An ancient fortress which is 3,000–3,200 years old and was built with the so-called Cyclopean masonry has been found [. . .] in Bulgaria's Rhodope Mountains, near the [. . .] border with Greece,

*Cadmus means the bright "east," and Europa is thought to derive from Semitic *erev* meaning "evening." Morning and evening stars appear and set in the east and west, respectively, so Cadmus and Europa were the twins of sunrise and sunset.

†The Mycenaeans, along with people from Crete, took part in the war against Troy and defeated the city with the ruse known as the Trojan horse. Troy is another story that helps to illustrate the runic secrets. The war began after Helen (wife of Menelaus, the king of Sparta) was stolen away to the labyrinth of Troy.

> and is taken as evidence that Ancient Thrace was part of the Mycenaean Civilization. The previously undetected fortress is roughly dated to 1,200 BC, i.e., to the time of Ancient Troy and the Trojan War.[7]

Phoenicians and Egyptians are closely associated with the Mystery traditions of Greece. According to mythology, the Thracian king Eumolpus, claimed by Greek historian Diodorus Siculus to be Egyptian, was thought to be the founder of the Eleusinian Mysteries. These, like other such myths, promised hope for a life after death. Celebrated for hundreds of years in Greece, these rites were based on the story of Persephone. The daughter of Demeter (one of the many names of Earth as goddess) had been carried away to the Underworld to stay for half the year while the sorrowing earth lay barren. Demeter's return to the world above represented the return of spring—and life.

Thor, a son of the earth goddess Jörd eventually traveled north from Thrace with the Norse gods known as the Aesir and Vanir, whom we will describe later in this book.

TRANSMISSION OF THE MYSTERIES

The early alphabet was often associated with craftsmen, such as potters and metalworkers, who apparently transmitted the alphabet informally:

> The isolated settings of these discoveries [. . .] suggests that writing was distributed through travel, the communication of mobile craftsmen. We will see extensive evidence of this two centuries later when traders spread the alphabet to the Greek world.[8]

Along with the alphabet, these craftsmen passed along the Mysteries, which in addition to promising enlightenment if not actual resurrection, transmitted such skills as winemaking, metallurgy, alchemy, mathematics, masonry, and astronomy.

The secrets of metalworking, like other Mysteries, were closely guarded by the initiates, and many of the earliest alphabet inscriptions were written on metal weapons. But although this new alphabet was primarily used to mark ownership, there is another path hiding among the symbols chosen to represent each letter, as I hope to demonstrate. This path, forgotten in the mists of time, was transmitted only to a few, possibly through initiation into the craftsmen guilds.

After acquiring the Semitic letters, the Greeks changed their names. Aleph as "ox" became the Greek letter alpha, Beth as "house" became beta, and so on. Although the early letter-objects were transformed into meaningless sounds, the Greeks acquired a form of Kabbalah which included numbered letters as gematria with multiple attributes for each letter. The later rune alphabets contain a similar versatility which will be described in detail in the upcoming chapters.

Symbols and Meanings of the Ancient Scripts

The tables that follow provide the symbols, names, and meanings of the Phoenician/Old Hebrew Alphabet as well as the Elder and the Younger Futharks. Our oldest alphabet, Phoenician/Old Hebrew gave names to each symbol. Runes (the FUThARKs), among other writing systems adapting the first alphabet, named their letter-symbols after their own word hoard. But significantly, they followed an identical path through the world of life and afterlife until a return to the light of earlier Mystery traditions.

PHOENICIAN/OLD HEBREW ALPHABET
(circa 1050 BCE)

Number	Symbol*	Name	Meaning
1	𐤀	Aleph	Ox
2	𐤁	Beth	House
3	𐤂	Gimel	Camel or rope
4	𐤃	Dalet	Door

PHOENICIAN/OLD HEBREW ALPHABET (*cont.*)

(circa 1050 BCE)

Number	Symbol*	Name	Meaning
5	𐤄	Hey	Window
6	𐤅	Wau	Nail
7	𐤆	Zain	Weapon
8	𐤇	Heth	Gate or fence
9	𐤈	Teth	Wheel or coil
10	𐤉	Yod	Hand
11	𐤊	Kaf	Palm of hand
12	𐤋	Lamed	Ox goad or rod of the teacher
13	𐤌	Mem	Water
14	𐤍	Nun	Serpent or fish
15	𐤎	Samekh	Prop or fish
16	𐤏	Ain	Eye
17	𐤐	Pe	Mouth or commandment
18	𐤑	Tsade	Hunt or fishhook
19	𐤒	Qopf	Monkey
20	𐤓	Ros	Head
21	𐤔	Shin	Tooth
22	𐤕	Tau	Mark

*Note: These are identical to the shapes of early Hebrew (Ketav Ivri).

ELDER FUTHARK RUNES

(circa 150–800 CE)

Number	Symbol	Name	Interpretation
1	ᚠ	Fehu, Feoh, Fe	Cattle or wealth
2	ᚢ	Uruz or Ur	Aurochs, ore, rain, or dross
3	ᚦ	Thurisaz or Thurs	Thorn or giant
4	ᚨ	Ansuz, Ass, or Os	High god or mouth
5	ᚱ	Raido, Rad, or Reið	Ride or wheel
6	ᚲ	Kenaz, Kaun, or Cen	Pine torch, ulcer, or canker
7	ᚷ	Gyfu	Gift
8	ᚹ	Wunjo or Wynn	Joy or white
9	ᚺ	Hagalaz	Hag god (Hel), hail, or heal
10	ᚾ	Naudiz or Nyd	Need
11	ᛁ	Isaz, Is, or Iss	Ice
12	ᛃ	Jera, Ger, or Ar	Harvest, plenty, or year
13	ᛇ	Ihwaz or Eihwaz	Yew tree
14	ᛈ	Perth	Lot or dice box
15	ᛉ	Algiz	Elk (horned deity) or elk sedge
16	ᛊ	Sowilo, Sol, or Sigel	Sun or victory
17	ᛏ	Tir, Tiwaz, or Tyr	God of the North Star

ELDER FUTHARK RUNES (*cont.*)

(circa 150–800 CE)

Number	Symbol	Name	Interpretation
18	ᛒ	Berkano, Beorc, or Bjarkan	Birch
19	ᛖ	Ehwaz or Eh	Horse
20	ᛗ	Mannaz	Man
21	ᛚ	Laguz, Logr, or Laukaz	Lake or leek
22	◇ ᛝ	Ingwaz	Earth god, also known as Ingvi-Frey
23	ᛞ	Dagaz	Day
24	ᛟ	Othala	Homeland or inheritance

YOUNGER FUTHARK RUNES

(circa 800–1100 CE)

Number	Symbol	Name	Interpretation
1	ᚠ	Fé	Wealth or money
2	ᚢ	Úr	Shadow, slag, or rain
3	ᚦ	Thurs	Giant
4	ᚨ	Óss	God or estuary
5	ᚱ	Reið	Ride
6	ᚴ	Kaun	Ulcer

YOUNGER FUTHARK RUNES (*cont.*)

(circa 800–1100 CE)

Number	Symbol	Name	Interpretation
7	ᚼ	Hagall	Hail
8	ᚾ	Nauðr	Need
9	ᛁ	Ísa/Íss	Ice
10	ᛅ	Ár	Plenty, good harvest, or year
11	ᛋ	Sól	Sun
12	ᛏ	Týr	One-handed god
13	ᛒ	Björk or Bjarkan	Birch
14	ᛘ	Maðr	Man or human
15	ᛚ	Lögr	Sea, water, or lake
16	ᛘ	Yr	Yew

Runes: A Mythic History

A thousand years after the Canaanites, now known as the Phoenicians, spread their alphabet, Germanic runes appeared. I am not implying here that runes evolved directly from the Phoenician alphabet, as there were undoubtedly intermediaries along the twisting path that the alphabets and alchemy traditions traveled. But understanding the pattern of our alphabet allows us to interpret the magic empowering runes. Like the Phoenician/Hebrew alphabet, runes use the first sounds of the letter-object to write their language. While rune symbols were chosen from their own culture, I hope to show they faithfully followed the path hiding within the alphabet's Mystery order.

BLACK SEA AREA: CELTS, GERMANS, EGYPTIANS, AND GREEKS

According to René Derolez in *Runica Manuscripta*, many scholars believe that runes are associated "with the settlement of the Goths [a Germanic people] in the Black Sea area."[1] Myth constantly diverges and converges with true history, and the Norse, recording their history, declared that the warrior god Odin acquired the runes in the lands of the goddess Asia, now known as Asia Minor. In this land Odin hung from the World Tree Yggdrasil for nine days to acquire the secrets of the runes.

"The country east of the Tanaquisl [the river Don] in Asia was called Asaland [. . .] and the chief city in that land was called Asgaard. In that city was a chief called Odin."[2] The river Don, flowing into the Sea of Asov, the northern extension of the Black Sea, was viewed as the border between Europe and Asia by ancient Greek geographers. A melting pot of cultures since before the early Bronze Age, this area attracted a parade of invaders and traders, including Scythians, Egyptians, Greeks, Romans, Tatars, Italians, Turks, Russians, and eventually the Norsemen. It was the center of a major trading route where mysteries and technologies, as well as trade goods, were exchanged.

Although the Norsemen are primarily remembered as pirates, the marauding Vikings developed extensive trade networks much like the earlier Phoenicians. Sweden and the Germanic Frisians had important commercial centers and trade guilds. They traded as far away as Britain, Greece and Byzantium in Turkey, and even along the Silk Road to China.

Following the thread through the labyrinth of myth into history, the goddess Asia (whose name translates as "resurrection") married Iapetus. Iapetus is identified with Japheth, son of Noah,* the biblical ancestor of the Greeks, Celts, and the Germanic peoples of Odin.

Before leaving Asia, Odin's people, the Aesir, fought a war with the Vanir, a family of fertile earth gods and goddesses. Described below, the Vanir taught Odin the art of travel through the Underworld.

> The power of the Vanir over the realm of the dead is associated with rebirth rather than with a journey to another world, as was the cult of Odin. Freyr [Vanir son of Earth, brother of Freya] was reborn in the person of each king, while at the same time the king who died was identified with the god in the earth [. . .] Here again there is an interesting parallel with the ritual of kingship [of] Ancient Egypt.[3]

---

*According to the *Oxford Classical Dictionary*, it is "far from unlikely that Iapetus and Japheth are the same person. Neither name is Greek or Hebrew, perhaps a shared tradition from an Anatolian source."

After making peace, they exchanged hostages. The Aesir sent the all-knowing Mimir along with a silent Hoenir in exchange. The Vanir sent Njord and his son Freyr along with Kvasir, their wisest, from whose blood the mead of poetry will be brewed: "They blended honey with the blood and the outcome was that mead by the virtue of which he who drinks becomes a skald or scholar."[4]

Believing they received a poor exchange in return for Kvasir, the Vanir cut off Mimir's head. Odin took the head, smeared it with herbs so that it would not rot, and sang charms over it. These gave the head the power to speak to him and tell him many secrets.[5] Thereafter, Odin expanded his powers by drinking from the mead of poetry. After drinking, he budded and became wise. "One word chased another word flowing from my mouth, one deed chased another deed flowing from my hands."[6]

Eventually, Odin built his great northern city of Valhalla which is supported by the great tree Yggdrasil holding nine realms above its three roots. Each root contains a well. Odin placed Mimir's head in the well of fate (Urd) in the land of the frost giants (Jotunheim). Before Mimir allowed Odin to drink knowledge from Urd's waters, he demanded the sacrifice of an eye, so Odin became the one-eyed god.

TROY SAGAS AND THE GOLDEN FLEECE STORIES

We tend to vastly underuse mythic stories in our modern search for historic truth, yet "true" historical connections can often be found in a culture's mythology. For instance, an early name for the Greeks, the Danaans, comes from an Egyptian colony run by Danaus. He had a twin brother named Aígyptos (Egypt) who had colonies around the Black Sea area of the goddess Asia. Danaus was another descendent of the cow goddess Isis/Hathor/Io/Balaat and the Nile. His cousin was the alphabet-bearing, Mystery-transmitting Phoenician Cadmus mentioned in the introduction.

The historian Herodotus claimed the people of Colchis, a kingdom near the Black Sea, were black-skinned Egyptians. Although outside the topics of this book, it's interesting to note that the land of Colchis hosted the adventures of the Argonauts and their search for a Golden Fleece. Their homeland was Thessaly, which was near Thrace. Thracians derive their name from the sorceress Thrace. Like Cadmus, her sister was Europa.[7] Allies of the Trojans, another famous Thracian is Orpheus. And like other initiates, Orpheus entered and returned from the Underworld (Orphic Mysteries). Astronomical knowledge hides in the Mysteries, Orpheus was son of Earth and Starry Heaven.

Some Thracians joined their adventure of the Golden Fleece and, on their way home, fought at the battle of Troy. In Norse tales recorded a thousand years later, Thor is identified as a prince of Troy from Thrace, and stories of Troy wander in and out of the sagas and histories. Stories about Troy and the Golden Fleece circulated throughout Europe early in the Common Era. The *Trojumanna saga* appeared in the North, circa 1250, about the time the *Prose Edda*, a collection of Norse mythological stories, was written.

Just south of Troy is the once important trade city of Miletus. It is situated along the trade route linking the Black Sea to Egypt and the islands of the Mediterranean. Around 1900 BCE, Minoans from Crete arrived. According to the Greek geographer Strabo (circa 64 BCE–20 CE): "Ephorus says: Miletus was first founded and fortified above the sea by Cretans, where the Miletus of olden times is now situated [. . . and colonists] from the Cretan Miletus [. . .] named the city after that Miletus."[8] Milesians, allies of the Trojans during their war against the Mycenaean Greeks, were the first to use the alphabet's number magic that became known as Gematria.

Some of the Greek sagas affecting many of the histories recounted by early northern scholars claimed that Odin himself came from Troy, which is in today's Turkey:

> From the north and over the eastern areas all to the south, this is called Asia. In the middle of the world. Here Odin constructed that building and residence which was called Troy. Having the gift of prophecy, Odin knew his name would be exalted in the northern

part of the world and glorified above all kings. Because of this he was keen to set off from Turkey.[9]

The ritual center of Troy, hiding a stolen maiden, fell to attacking Greeks circa 1200 BCE. Virgil believes people from Crete first established Troy. After its destruction, "The Walls of Troy were rebuilt by [. . .] architects of Crete after the model of the Cretan Labyrinth which was an exact representation of the stellar universe."[10]

By the time the *Prose Edda* was compiled (circa 1201–1300 CE), not only Odin, but multiple peoples claimed descent from Troy. Possibly influenced by Greek works entering Europe by way of Arab translators, stories of the Trojan war had circulated widely in Europe since early in the Common Era. The Merovingian Franks claimed Trojan ancestors. Virgil's *Aeneid* described a Trojan prince founding Rome, and turf mazes called Troy Town mazes began appearing throughout Europe, which resembled the maze-like structure of Troy's walls.

Greece, Crete, Phoenicia, the Black Sea area, and Egypt have a long history together, including shared mathematics, masonry, astronomy, medicine, divination, and writing, to be explored in the upcoming chapters.

THREE COMMON RUNIC SCRIPTS

The rune scripts, or futharks, adopted few shapes or sounds of the original alphabet, but like their ancestor, each letter names an object and all are in a set order. The three common runic orders are the Elder Futhark with twenty-four runes (circa 150–800 CE), the Anglo-Saxon Futhark (also known as the Old English Futhark) with twenty-eight runes (circa 400–1100 CE), and the Younger Futhark with sixteen runes (circa 800–1100 CE). The Anglo-Saxon (Old English) runes repeat the twenty-four runes of the Elder Futhark but end with some additional figures. Details on each of the runes of the Elder and Younger Futharks, as well as the letters of the Phoenician/Hebrew alphabet, can be found in the previous chapter, "Symbols and Meanings of the Ancient Scripts."

Like the alphabet named for its first two letters—alpha and beta—the futhark is named for the magical "hex" of the first six letters: Fehu (cattle), Uruz (aurochs), Thurisaz (thorn), Ansuz (high god), Raido (ride), and Kenaz (torch): FUThARK.

The earliest known runes are the twenty-four letters of the Elder Futhark. Appearing in short inscriptions around the beginning of the Common Era, all twenty-four appeared in the present order around 400 CE on the Kylver stone, a limestone slab found in a tomb in Sweden.

Being interested in the myths rather than in the epigraphy of runes, I am seldom concerned with the various shapes of these letters. I purposely ignore them because modern scholars tend to fixate on differences between the shapes and sounds of runes and their ancient ancestors, Phoenician and Old Hebrew. To understand the choice of objects representing runes, they need to comprehend the similarity of the *mythic* qualities of the ordered objects, the shared pattern which illustrates the futhark.

MYTHS AND MYSTERIES OF THE RUNES

Along with the technology of an alphabet, the Norse acquired alchemical secrets through the runes. Carved and painted, the runes' very name—*rune* meaning "secret"—hints at the Mysteries hiding in their order: "At the origin [runes] were probably a secret craft, if the interpretation of [. . .] 'run' as a secret, mystery, etc. is to have any value."[11]

Without some basic understanding of the knowledge available to ancient scholars, we dismiss their observations. As Gisli Sigurdsson says, "This oldest scientific knowledge of mankind is no longer part of general education in Western cultures, not even among the university educated elite which specializes in understanding texts of old."[12] But that arrogance is beginning to change as we learn more about the depths of ancient science.

Runes, like all Mysteries, hide knowledge of both earth and sky among their order. *The Saga of the Volsungs* "tells of the origin of runes and seems to contain another fragment relating to the signs of the heavens and the mysterious characters which they trace on the black vault of a moonless night, a fancy which the Jewish cabalists shared."[13]

Runes were seldom used for writing stories, but rather were primarily employed to mark ownership, used for magic and divination, and inscribed on boundary markers, stones, or bridges erected for the dead. This suggests a belief that runes facilitated a passage between borders, such as that between the living and the dead. The secrets hidden in the runes of northern Europe, like all great Mystery traditions, once described a circling back from a grave ending. Old traditions recall a grave from which the dead once returned in their season before it became an old wife's tale. Although later users forgot the older promise, Othala ᛟ, the last of twenty-four early runes, was once a welcoming homeland.

It was once believed that men who died were born again. One example is the story of two lovers, the hero Helgi and the Valkyrie Sigrun. After Helgi was killed, Sigrun rode to his burial mound to lie with him. The sorrowing Sigrun mourned, "I have made thee a bed here, Helgi, a very painless bed, thou son of the Wolfings. I shall sleep in thine arms, O king, as I should if thou wert yet alive."[14]

Sigrun died from sorrow shortly after, but the lovers were said to have been born again: Sigrun as Cara and Helgi as the ruler of the Hadding clan.[15] Cara, like her predecessor Sigrun, was a witch wife, a Valkyrie taking the shape of a swan flying into battle. Many references appearing in runic traditions contain the story of the cursed lovers, who also appear as Siegfried/Sigurd and Sigrdrifa/Brynhild. We will encounter the Haddings again in our discussion of the rune Ingwaz.

Other Mysteries inherent in the runes are linked to number magic. The number twenty-four, for example, commonly appears: there are twenty-four books in Homer's *Odyssey* through the heavens and twenty-four vertebrae in the spine that India's serpent-goddess climbs toward enlightenment (Kundalini). As a calendar marker, there are twenty-four hours in an Egyptian day—the number of bright and dark fortnights measured by the moon during the twelve months of the solar year. The potent full moon falls on the fifteenth day of each lunar circle (360/15 = 24). After dying into the black, the new moon returns brightly young, and after midnight, the dark sun will return as a shining new day.

There is never just one origin or one explanation for myths. Each source adds to the power of the story. Another example, the power of twenty-four is associated with a cycle of Mars, known as Tir (Tues) in the northern world. Spinning out Time (said to begin on the third day of Tuesday), Mars loops "around the zodiac in seven steps, returning to the area where the first loop was made with the eighth loop. This cycle takes fifteen years and once every fifteen years the planet is particularly brilliant"[16] (360/15 = 24).

Magic charms relating directly to rune numbers can be found throughout the myths. For instance, Time begins when the "pricks" of the arrow-shooting rulers of the third symbol bind Earth's red flood in pregnancy: "This Third I chant thee: if great waters threaten to overwhelm thee, may flood and foam [. . .] dry up before thee."[17] And after her bonds are loosened, Earth delivers her new world through the mouth of the fourth rune, Oss. Odin, adapting birth magic to a warrior's use declaims, "I know a fourth spell; one if chains and locks are placed upon my limbs, I cast this spell so that I can escape. The chains burst from my hands; the locks burst from my feet."[18]

These are just a few of the many types of secrets and Mysteries inherent in the runes. We will discover many more relating to each rune in turn in the upcoming chapters.

SOURCES OF RUNIC INFORMATION

Throughout this book, I follow the path of the runes by watching for clues dropped by earlier writers. I sift through and compare numerous patterns from vastly different cultures, starting with the first transmitters of the alphabet: the Phoenicians.

The twenty-four runes of the Elder Futhark provide my main template but unlike later traditions, they have no mnemonic poems to describe them. These rune poems provide an explanatory poetic stanza for each letter of the later rune traditions and are among the main sources for understanding each letter's position. They also help to flesh out the attributes of the objects representing the twenty-four older letters.

The poems include the Old Icelandic Rune Poem (OIRP) recorded in late fifteenth century, the Old Norwegian Rune Poem (ONRP) from the early thirteenth century, and the Old English Rune Poem (OERP) from the ninth century. The modern English versions I quote throughout the book come primarily from the Bruce Dickins translation, unless otherwise noted. Important to our understanding is the Old Icelandic Rune poem, which differs from the other two sources. After its appearance, an anonymous scribe added glosses* to clarify the symbolism and meaning behind the poem. Many English translations of the poem do not include the glosses. I have added the transliterated Icelandic which include the glosses as they are critical to an exploration of the rune meanings.

In the later futharks, the number of runes was decreased to sixteen (Younger Futhark) or increased to twenty-eight (Anglo-Saxon/Old English). While reducing the number of letters made the futharks less useful for writing speech, the new positions kept the symbolism implied by the earlier ones. And although the changes in number undoubtedly held a mystical meaning for the scholars who made them, I found no information on their reason for doing so. In any case, the first six runes, the magical hex, remained the same: F-U-Th-A-R-K.

In addition to the poems, I investigate numerous patterns in palmistry, astrology, Celtic oghams, and children's rhymes containing memories of older rituals for each rune to further our understanding of the attributes underlying the number magic of the ancient alphabets and their associated objects. I also explore other numbered stories, including such tales as the nine ordered verses a dead mother recites to her son, a numbered series of directions a Valkyrie gives to her lover, and the knowledge of the eighteen charms with which Odin taunts a defeated dragon. I also include *Grimner's Lay* where Odin describes twelve Halls, each occupied by a god.

---

*Glosses are explanatory words or phrases written by later scribes in the poems that act as translations or definitions that help to explain the overall meaning of each rune.

Understanding the attributes associated with each physical object described by the early alphabet translates into an understanding of why the runes chose their objects a thousand years later. It also becomes clear that runes follow the orderly pattern of the older-alphabet spell. They tell of a journey through life, death, and a return into light, containing calendar secrets based on the turning Earth and—as above so below—mirrored by her sky.

ODIN'S DISTRIBUTION OF THE RUNES

Having acquired the runes, the High One inscribed them:

> [. . .] on the bear's paw, on Brage's tongue, on the Wolf's claw, and the Eagle's beak, on the bloody wings, and the Bridge's end; on the midwife's palm, on the healing foot-print, on men's amber and gold, on talismans, on wine and wort, and the Sibyl's seat; on Gungni's point, and Grani's breast; on the Norn's nail, and the owl's beak.—All that were engraven were scraped off and mixed with holy mead and sent away on every side. The Anses [Odin's Aesir] have some, the Elves have some, some the wise Wanes [Vanir] have; mortal men have some.[19]

Brage is the Norse god of poetry. When Odin seduced Gunlodd, the daughter of a giant guarding the mead of poetry, she gave birth to their son, Brage. After stealing the mead, Odin broke his oath to marry her. Like other oath-breakers, he will die on the Day of the Wolf when the giants ride over the great bridge of heaven.

While Norse Vikings were not averse to slaughter and theft in search of riches, honor was important, leading to the death of all oath-breakers in the sagas. The Sibyl (known in the North as a Volva or seer) prophesizes the wind-age, the wolf-age of Ragnarok when the old gods die.[20] Gungni is Odin's enchanted spear. Never missing its mark, along with the gods, it is destroyed when the giant wolf breaks loose from his fetters to destroy Odin.

One further explanation about the "healing footprint": Germans swore binding oaths upon their soles. "On entering upon a league [brotherhood], the ancients were wont to soak their footprints with a mutual aspersion of gore, that their pledges of friendliness might be established by the blending of their blood."[21]

It has been asserted that the peculiar arrangement of the twenty-four runes of the Elder Futhark betrays a "mnemonic device that is no longer retrievable, but which may have left some slight echo in the runic poems preserved in medieval manuscripts."[22] I believe the original Mystery, transmitted secretly by these symbols and deliberately obscured, once sought to guide the soul toward enlightenment. The many hints found among these sources make our retrieval quite possible.

The Rune Families

Freyr, Hel, and Tir

Three Families of Runes

By at least the sixth century, the runes appear arranged in three *aettir*—or families headed by Freyr, Hel, and Tir—each having eight runes. Even after the Futhark was reduced to 16, the family groups remained.*[1]

FREYR

The first group begins with Freyr (a.k.a. Frodi), the god of the earth, and reflects a cycle of fertility, growth, and harvest, and then a rising up into a new light—the joy of white Wynn, the eighth rune. In the North, under Freyr's golden reign, Earth knew peace and good harvests.

HEL

The second family begins with Hel, goddess of the Underworld. Her eight runes describe a soul journey after death and an emergence once more into the light of day, into the sun: Sol, the sixteenth rune. The Phoenician/Hebrew alphabet ancestor of the runes begins Hel's family with the ninth letter, Teth, meaning "clew" or "coil,"† the thread helping heroes navigate this Underworld.

---

*The families appear on the Vadstena & Grumpan Bracteates—gold pendants with runic inscriptions dating from approximately fifth–sixth centuries BCE.

†A clew is "a ball of thread used especially with reference to the thread supposedly used by Theseus to mark his way out of the Cretan labyrinth" (*The Oxford Dictionary*); "a ball of thread, yarn, or cord," or "something that guides through an intricate procedure or maze of difficulties" (*Merriam-Webster Dictionary*).

TIR

The third family begins with Tir, the seventeenth rune. Associated with the command of stars spinning around the North Star, Tir's family includes more astronomical data. Following this pattern is Greek Pi (π), commanding the area of the circle, and the Hebrew Pe, meaning "mouth" or "commandment," as the seventeenth symbol. As the command of the North Star was changing, there was a period when no star was the Nail of the Sky. The Norse god Tir held his hand in this ravenous "mouth," keeping control until a new ruler captured the circling stars, saving the world from collapse.

We end as the twenty-fourth and final rune returns to earth as womb-shaped Othala (homeland). The Phoenician/Hebrew alphabet ends with the Tav, meaning "mark," which, like the mark of Cain, promises that death will pass over. Most rune lore comes from Christian scholars transmitting a pagan world they didn't understand and only occasionally admired. Thus, although the futhark may once have hidden an alchemist's promise of enlightenment, by the time of the rune poems, several hundred years after runes first appeared, the symbols had been transmuted into a warrior's magic that eventually ends in a grave:

The grave is horrible to every knight,
when the corpse quickly begins to cool
and is laid in the bosom of the dark earth.
Prosperity declines,
happiness passes away,
and covenants are broken.

OLD ENGLISH RUNE POEM

First Aettir

Freyr's Family

Mother Goose's song reflects the mysteries hiding among the runes:

One for sorrow, Two for mirth,
Three for a wedding, Four for a birth,
Five for silver, Six for gold,
Seven's a story ne're to be told.

MOTHER GOOSE DIVINATION POEM

FREYR'S RUNES

Number	Name	Meaning
1	Fehu, Feoh, or Fe	Cattle or wealth
2	Uruz or Ur	Aurochs, ore, rain, or dross
3	Thurisaz or Thurs	Thorn or giant
4	Ansuz, Ass, Oss	High god or mouth
5	Raido, Rad, or Reidh	Ride or wheel
6	Kenaz, Kaun, or Cen	Pine torch, ulcer, or canker
7	Gyfu	Gift
8	Wunjo or Wynn	Joy, white

The first eight runes belong to the earth god, the generous Freyr (a.k.a. Frodi). One of the Vanir, the family of fertile earth gods and goddesses, he traveled north with Odin and Thor to Scandinavia. Under the prosperity of the first aettir, we are born, marry, have children, and reap the peace and plenty of a material world. After midsummer's prime, our spirits die south toward the fall of man.

1. Fehu

Cattle or Wealth

Variants: Feoh or Fe (ᚠ)

Wealth (Feoh) is a comfort to all men; yet must every man bestow it freely, if he wish to gain honour in the sight of the Lord.

Old English Rune Poem

*Wealth (Fe) source of discord among kinsmen and fire of the sea, and path of the serpent.**

Fé er frænda róg, ok flæðar viti, ok grafseiðs gata, aurum fylkir.
Glosses: *Aurum* (gold), *fylkir* (king or leader)

Old Icelandic Rune Poem

One for the money

Mother Goose nursery rhyme

*Path of the serpent also translates as "path of the grave fish," a reference to the dragon hoarding gold in graves.

THE UNDIVIDED ONE

Fehu (meaning wealth or cattle) is the first rune. It offers the promise of a fertile Earth's golden bounty: "Feoh id est pecunia."*[1]

The first position in our ancient Mystery belongs to an undivided *One*. It is not until One separates into duality that the cascade toward the material world ensues. Entering the material world, the traveler also enters the world of time and death, the fee paid by the living: "One for sorrow" is another of Mother Goose's memories.

The first letter of the ancient alphabet is Aleph, meaning "ox," a castrated animal, making it a nonsexual creature. Young One has not yet separated with adolescence. When sexuality emerges with duality and One becomes Two, multitudes emerge. Our letter *A* is the shape of a woman's womb out of which the path of life begins and of cow-shaped motherly graves from which the dead hoped to return. The word *Fe* is suggestive of an androgynous fairy or *fey*, similar to Aleph's nonsexual ox. This fey One stands at the boundary between the worlds.

The wealth of the material world appears as life on Earth unfolds. Vikings sought wealth when they went a-Viking, either as merchants or as pirates. The Norse, encouraged to share their gold—their *pecunia*—among their companions, were also warned against becoming materialistic.

Fig. 1. Cash Cow as A to T (first and last letters of the ancient alphabet).

Harold Bayley, *Lost Language of Symbolism* (1912) [Rowman and Littlefield, 1968], 102.

*The gloss pecunia (money) is by a 16th century hand.

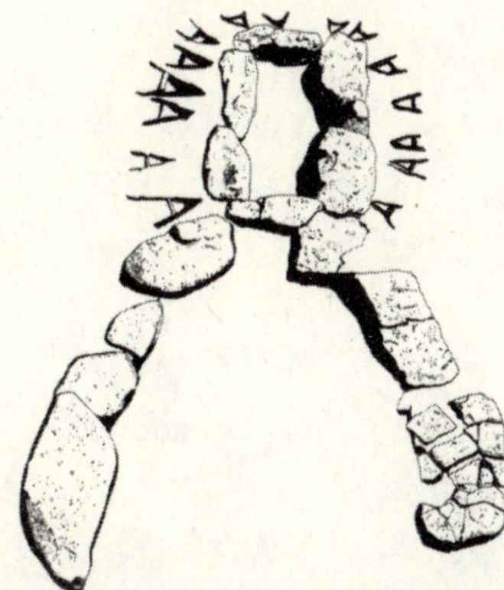

Fig. 2. Grave in the form of an A. Yugoslavia, circa 6000 BCE.

From Gimbutas, *The Language of the Goddess*, 156.

FE: Wealth is a source of discord among kinsmen; the wolf lives in the forest.

OLD NORWEGIAN RUNE POEM

THE PRECESSION AND KNOWLEDGE OF THE STARS

As in early Greek tales by Homer about his Trojan war, the cycles of stars and heavenly bodies wander in and out of Norse sagas and rune poems. Knowledge of their measurements were important secrets empowering scholars of ancient Mysteries.

Earth has a slight wobble in her orbit, which results in a slow backward precession of the North Pole shining below the North Star. Known as the precession of the equinoxes, the wobble causes stars rising on the spring equinox to slowly migrate backward through the sky. After an entire turn on the wheel, the center of the sky marked by the polestar returns to its original position.

Once among the stars of the dragon Draco, after passing through an empty place in the sky, the polestar migrated toward the Wagons (the Dippers). Because of this wobble, the dragon no longer ruled the sky. He had lost his position as Nail of the North. Odin, known by many names, including Irmin and Jormunr, become the new ruler. Centuries later Charlemagne destroyed Odin's great tower, the Irminsul, and took control of the polar stars, which were renamed Charles's Wains.

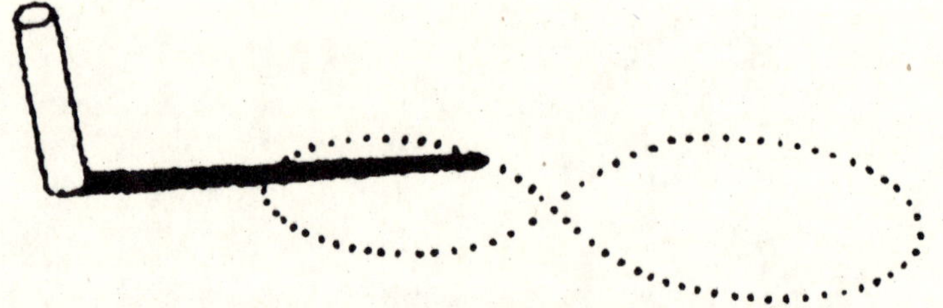

Fig. 3. Herm as a sundial tracing a year's shadow.
Illustrator Unknown.

HERMES THE GUIDE

In many traditions, young Mercury/Hermes performs the role of the guide, the pathfinder between the boundaries of life and death. Hermes began life as a simple herm—a pillar like numeral 1 that was used to designate boundaries. He is associated with trade, wealth, and the shared knowledge these enabled. As a herm at the boundary between light and dark, he traces the shadow of the bright sun throughout infinity (see Fig. 3 above). The shadow's shape has become the mathematical symbol for infinity.

One of the many traditions about the creation of the alphabet states Hermes invented the letters. Odin, who acquired his runes near the Black Sea, is identified as a warrior form of Hermes. In Egypt, the god Thoth, judge of the dead as they enter the Underworld—another boundary between the material and the ethereal—is also credited with inventing writing. The Greeks identified Thoth with Hermes, and as the Thrice Great Thoth, he morphed into the legendary figure of Hermes Trismagistus—credited with writing the Hermetica.

Warriors, Pathfinders, and Pirates

> *There are Beech-runes, Help-runes, Love-runes, and great Power-runes, for whomsoever will, to have for charms [. . .] till the world falls in ruin. Profit by them if thou canst.*
>
> Corpus Poeticum Boreale,
> Vigfusson and Powell trans.

In the following chant of the High One, Odin sings the first of eighteen spells to taunt a defeated dragon Loddfafnir: "I counsel thee, Stray-Singer, accept my counsels, they will be thy boon if thou obey'st them" [. . .] I know songs, such as no King's daughter, nor son of man knows. HELP the first is called."[2]

Although North men were wide-ranging traders as well as pirates, Odin was primarily a warrior's god. Rather than Odin, Thor who came from Thrace was the source of help— the pathfinder evoked for family protection. Along with the three rune poems, there are several other stories fleshing out Mysteries hiding among the runes.

In The Lay of Grimnir, whose subject is celestial geometry,[3] the halls of the gods are described. Thor's home is in the First Hall. "Thor shall ever in Thrudheim [Thrace] dwell, Till the gods to destruction go."[4] His Hall has 540 doors. 800 warriors will emerge on the Day of the Wolf and "the gods 'to destruction go.'" (800 × 540 = 432,000). This number signifying the end of time has appeared in numerous traditions including Babylonian, Hebrew, and Indian.

It may be folk etymology, but Thor, a thunder god invoked for fertility and help, also appears as Tor. A *tor* is a tower, a high-seat pillar,* or the herm described as numeral 1. As a taur (bull) he recalls Aleph's symbolism of the ox and the fey guide as pathfinder.

In another story from Groa's Chant, a young man setting out on a dangerous journey wakes his mother from her grave to ask for her advice. As we continue our journey, the words from this story ring true: "The first charm I chant thee [. . .] let thyself be thy guide."[5] Advising him to choose his own path, one's choice was later considered a heresy.†

*High-seat pillars were two poles of wood, or tors if you will, that were dedicated to Thor and sometimes carved with his image. Vikings sailing to new homes would take their pillars with them and throw them overboard near land. The new home was established where Thor's pillars washed up onshore.

†Most but not all Groa's charms follow the alphabet pattern.

2. Uruz or Ur

Wild Bull, Aurochs,* or Water (ᚢ)

Variants: Ore, rain, or dross

THE SECOND RUNE

Aurochs (Uruz) is proud and has great horns; it is a very savage beast and fights with its horns; a great ranger of the moors, it is a creature of mettle."

Old English Rune Poem

The aurochs as the second rune, Uruz was prized for its huge horns, which were used as ale cups: "The Germani collect them eagerly, encase their edges in silver, and use them as beakers at their most magnificent banquets."[1] They were thought to protect the drinker from poison, especially when inscribed with special runes. Similarly, in the Middle Ages the second finger, Apollo's finger, was thought to be able to detect poisons and was used for applying medicines. Also called the leechman, ringman or lickpan, there is said to be an artery that runs up the palm to this finger, connecting it directly with the heart. Thus, the taster could immediately sense the presence of poison.[2]

*A giant wild ox, now extinct.

ARRIVAL OF SEXUALITY: FROM THE SINGLE COMES THE MANY

[One] is not a number but is a producer (or mother), the beginning and foundation of all other numbers.

JACOB KOBEL, *RECHENBUCH* (1514)

Ancient authors considered odd numbers male and even numbers as female. Although one is odd, it was considered both male and female like the androgynous ox as aleph or the fey first rune.[3] When undivided One becomes Two, male from female separates as the child matures. Sexuality arrives with the appearance of their red and white waters, and the adolescent virgins must be purified and prepared for their coming role as fertile adults. The Hebrew tradition concurs with Psalm 119:9, which asks, [Beth] "Wherewithal shall a young man cleanse his way?" Both male and female need purification after their waters appear (Latin, *februa*, "to clean" from which our second month of February is derived) The land must be readied for plowing in all its farming and sexual connotations.

The second Phoenician/Old Hebrew letter Beth means "house," and a *betulah* in Hebrew is a young virgin. Ancient festivals were often celebrated by virgins worshipping the goddess by the central hearth. The vestal virgins, priestesses of the Roman goddess Vesta (whose name is thought to derive from the Greek *hestia*, meaning "hearth"), kept the sacred fire going. Celtic women supplied many brides to the far-roving Vikings. The festival of Ireland's Bride, also known as Imbolc or Saint Brigid's Day, is celebrated in early February by the fireplace. On this night the Hag returns as the Virgin Spring and maidens looking for February's valentines hope to discover their mates.

With the arrival of duality, two's story includes healing energy, inspiration, learning, and wisdom; far travel, frenzy, ecstasy, and strength also appear. It is during the stormy tempests of adolescence that the virgin's waters emerge, signaling the moment for initiation into adulthood.

Young men must also be initiated into manhood before they can seed a new generation. With the arrival of sexuality, the male and his twin enter the ring, the clan, joining the circle of their village. The Old English Rune Poem quoted previously links the initiation rites of adolescent males to the aurochs, the second rune. According to Julius Caesar in *Conquest of Gaul*, the aurochs were hunted by Germanic youths: "This arduous sport toughens the young men and keeps them in training."[4]

Healing and Divination

> *I know a second spell which men need if they want to heal others.*
>
> "HAVAMAL," CRAWFORD TRANS.

Healing belongs among the powers of the second charm. One of the problems facing a Western scholar is the firm belief that a symbol has finite definitions. Older peoples appreciated a looser approach. The powers of healing and divination are associated with young virgins: A virgin delivered the oracles of Delphi founded by Apollo and people from Crete. February, our second month, was the correct time to seek the Oracle's advice: "Originally the oracle delivered its pronouncements on [Apollo's birthday, the month] being approximately the equivalent of February."[5] That is, the virginal twins, Artemis and Apollo, are among those associated with the growing light of February.

THE MANY FACES OF UR

The primal rune Ur mandates flexibility if one is to resolve its seeming contradictions. There are overlays and underlays of meaning hiding beneath the objects of rune image. Ur is a multi-headed hydra. In addition to some of the meanings mentioned above, it can mean gold (aur), ore, fire, water, or young, as in primal. It can represent an aurochs with its horns used for drinking, auras of divination, and the arts of brewing: the making of fire (ur)-water (also ur).

One rune manuscript glossed the second Ur rune with the Latin word *noster*, meaning "our."[6] While this is technically an incorrect translation of the Ur rune, the writer is correct in his association. By Christian times, the Lord's Prayer, or Paternoster (Our Father), had become an important healer's charm: a nostrum written out, dissolved in liquid, and drunk.

Metallurgy

> *Dross (Ur) comes from bad iron; the reindeer often races over the frozen snow.*
>
> Old Norwegian Rune Poem

Along with healing and initiation rites, Ur hides important secrets of the ores of metallurgy. The earliest Canaanite alphabets in Egypt are associated with metalworkers: the "sons of the furnace' (bn kr), whose 'equipment' ('nt), notably the 'melt-furnace' (kbšn mš), features strongly in the inscriptions, and the remains of such metallurgical apparatus have been found on the site."[7] Phoenician Cadmus on his way to Greece may have been initiated into the mysteries of Cabeiri, which included metalworking dwarves, who are also associated with miners in Scandinavia.

A warrior's weapons were originally made from bronze, a mixture of tin and copper. Earth's iron was too soft to make a good weapon until men learned to harden and purify it. Purification being one theme of our second charm when ore (Ur) is purified by fire (Ur) and water (Ur), slag/dross (also Ur) remains. In the art of alchemy, dross (Ur) is purified into gold (aur), a blackened soul into the shining auras of enlightenment.

Trees and Rising Sap

> *From it come the dews that fall in the valleys. It stands forever green above Weird's [Urdr's] Well.*
>
> "Gylfaginning," in *Edda*,
> Anthony Faulkes trans.

Festivals celebrating trees also occur in early February, and spring-rising sap is used for brewing. The drinking horn could also be described in terms of a tree—the horns of the ox skull being the bent branches. Some cultures celebrating the New Year of the Trees include Tu B'Shvat—a Jewish tradition—and the Hindu holiday of Shivaratri. The February festival for Brigid, the Bride of Ireland mentioned earlier, is also celebrated along with the sap-rising trees. Brigid was a midwife, a brewer of ale, a metalsmith, and during her festival the fires of the smith were blessed.

Trees were celebrated for their energy of healing and renewal. The World Tree, the most famous tree of the northern world, has three roots supporting it, each with its own well: Urd, home of three fate-casting Norns; Mimir's well in the land of the Jotunheim (frost giants); and Hvergelmir (bubbling spring) in the ninth realm belonging to Hel. Urd, like Scandinavian Var, is a fate goddess, her name cognate with Wyrd (Weird). Above Urd's well, the World Tree's sap rises up the tree, dripping their sapience down from above to revitalize the land.

I sing you the second spell,
in case you must travel roads against your will,
then may Urd's bonds (Urðar lokur)
hold you on all sides,
while you are on the way.

"Groa's Chant," in *Edda*,
Anthony Faulkes trans.

Trees and their branches were also used in spells to protect and heal, and to curse:

Runes of branches [limrunar] thou must know,
if thou wilt be a leech,
and learn to search a wound.
Thou shalt grave them on the bark,
and on the stock of a tree whose branches lean eastwards.

Corpus Poeticum Boreale,
Vigfusson and Powell trans.

Never loathe to use magic to curse an enemy, a northern witch had another use for the healer's limrunar. She "carved runes into the root of a tree, reddening them with her own blood and reciting spells over them to bring disaster."[8] Odin, singing his charms in the words of the High One, counters the curse: "If a man wounds me by spells of a [. . .] tree; the curse shall bite him that lays the spells upon me rather than me."[9]

THE BRIDE OF FEBRUARY

Shower (Ur) lamentation of the clouds and ruin of the hay-harvest, and abomination of the shepherd.

Úr er skýja grátr ok skára þverrir ok hirðis hatr. umbre vísi.
Glosses: *Umbre* (shadow), *vísi* (leader)

Old Icelandic Rune Poem

In our second month of February Earth is young, a virginal spring, the bride having renewed herself during her dark winter. Her festivals are celebrated after winter's icy pause. Scandinavia's bride is Skadi. Her name, like that of dark moist female yin of China, translates as "shadow" and represents the northern realms. Traveling the frozen north with her wolves, Skadi is also known as Var, the name of the season of spring in the old Norse calendar. Var (spring) began the second full moon after winter, usually in February.

Winter is coldest, spring frostiest—it is longest cold.

"Maxims II," Anglo Saxon season

Uller's Nine Magic Twigs

In "Grimnismal," Odin describes the halls of his kingdom, and each was occupied by a god. Glorious Uller (Wuldor) lives in the Second Hall. Associated with the shadow bride, Skadi, Uller may once have been a healer. Although most of Uller's stories are lost, Odin borrowed his nine healing twigs: "Then took [Odin] nine magic twigs (*wuldortanas*); then smote the serpent that in nine bits dispersed."[10]

The nine herbs were said to have been borrowed by Odin to dispel the serpents of sickness. A nine-herb charm appears in the Anglo-Saxon Lacnunga text.* The charm names nine herbs that may have been inscribed with runes on their twigs to work their magic (Odin's runes were placed "on talismans, on wine and wort").

The first and oldest, *Artemesia vulgaris*, or mugwort, was sacred to Artemis: "Remember, Mugwort [. . .] You were called Una, the oldest of herbs."[11] Mugwort (Artemisia vulgaris) is also related to wormwood (Artemisia absinthium). This is the green fairy used in making the psychoactive drink absinthe, which is effective against worms.

Rings and Oaths

> *I counsel thee secondly: Swear no oath, except it be true.*
>
> "Sigrdrifumal,"
> Vigfusson and Powell trans.

Rings and oaths arrive with this second charm along with divination and healing powers. The young virgins of February will soon exchange their rings and enter the marriage bed. In the tradition of palmistry, the second finger (Apollo's finger) is the ring finger where wedding rings are placed. Uller was the keeper of the temple rings on which Vikings swore oaths: "By the southing sun, the Great God's rock, the lintels of the bedchamber, and the ring of Wuldor."[12] The ring keeper shares the Second Hall with Freyr. Bringing peace and fertility to his land, Freyr was a frequent recipient of sacrifices giving the blessing of a wedding.

> In Norse mythology, Vár or Vór meaning either "pledge" or "beloved" is a goddess associated with oaths and agreements [. . .] she listens to people's oaths and private agreements that women and men make between each other. Thus these contracts are called *varar*. She also punishes those who break them.[13]

*This text can be found in the British Library's eleventh-century Harley 585 manuscript.

Described above, Skadi, wise god-bride, was also known as "bow-stung Var." Like wolfish Nemesis, mother of the virginal twins Artemis and Apollo, Var, in the company of her wolves, punished oath breakers. Our word *beware* and the German word for truth, *wahr*, comes from the goddess Vargr (wolf). Demanding *wergeld** in payment for spilling blood within her circle, the breaker of her peace, was evicted from the clan: a lone wolf in the forest no longer under her protective eye.

On the Day of the Wolf, the realm of the Northern gods will end, and a wolf will kill the oath-breaker Odin. He had broken his promise of marriage to Gundfled in exchange for help stealing a giant's precious mead: "a ring-oath Woden swore to Gundfled and broke."[14] Although it didn't save him from the wolf, he defended his action by claiming the mead stole his wits: "The crane called Forgetfulness lingers over the carousal of ale-drinking, it steals people's wits; with this bird's feathers I was fettered in the courtyard of Gunnlöð."[15]

Siegfried and the Ring Sword

Then second I rede thee,
to swear no oath
If true thou knowest it not;
Bitter the fate of the breaker of troth,
And poor is the wolf of his word.

"Sigrdrifumal,"
Henry Adams Bellows trans.

Finally, we tie together gods and goddesses traveling with wolves, metallurgy, oaths, and oath rings. Viking warriors began carrying ring swords between the sixth and seventh centuries CE: "The ultimate symbol of the social code was the ring sword . . . a weapon with a literal gold ring locked into its hilt."[16] These swords were prestigious possessions, probably reserved for kings and high nobility. The small ring attached to their hilt is interpreted as a symbolic "oath ring."

*Wergeld is the custom of requiring a murderer to pay a fine to the family of the victim.

The hero Siegfried, the dragon slayer, whose story appears frequently among the rune poems, owned such a ring sword, which he lay in the bed he shared with the Valkyrie Brynhild (Sigrdrifa). Having ridden through a ring of fire to woo Brynhild, he had given her a ring and sworn his love. However, he was given a draft of forgetfulness and was tricked into marriage with another woman, so he does not keep his oath. Like all northern oath breakers, his actions ultimately led to his death.

Fig. 4. Detail of ring sword.
From 7th century Gutenstein "Wolf Warrior" scabbard.
Photo by Schristian Bickel. Replica from Central Museum, Mainz (original from Pushkin Museum).

3. Thurs

Giant or Thorn

Variants: *Thurisaz, Thurisa* (Þ)

(Thorn) is exceedingly sharp, an evil thing for any knight to touch, uncommonly severe on all who sit among them.

Old English Rune Poem

FERTILITY AND FOOLS

While Thurisaz and Thurs (as thorn and giant) seem to have little in common to a modern reader, the thorn is a sharp "prick," with all its phallic references.

Number secrets underlie some of the alphabet symbols. Three, like thorn, represents a triangular number, which is a number that can be represented in the form of triangle. Every successive row contains one more element than the previous one. For instance, when as single dot is placed on one line and two dots are placed below it on a second line, it forms the shape of a triangle. Six, ten, fifteen, and twenty-one are also triangular numbers. All these positions have overt associations with fertility, which we shall explore when we discuss those rune positions.

Three's rune ᚦ is a fertile triangular number, the shape of a warrior's arrowhead. While most rune symbols came from a northern stock of

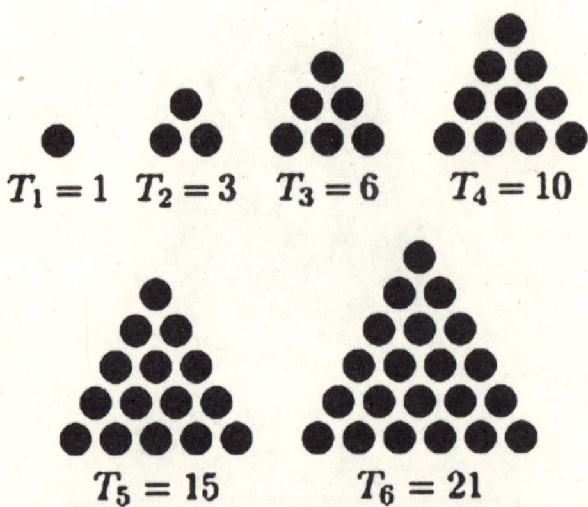

Fig. 5. First six triangular numbers.
Diagram by Melchoir.

symbols, the third rune was apparently adapted from Phoenician letter twenty-two, Ros meaning "head" ◅. Since Thurisaz is "marked [. . .] by [its] stupidity,"*[1] Three's one-eyed "head" belongs to a fool. "I counsel thee thirdly: Do not plead in court against an ignorant man: for a fool may drop worse words than he knows of."[2] The sexual symbolism of the foolish one-eyed "head" should be as obvious as those of thorns, arrows, rampant stallions, and lightening serpents entering the springtime furrows of a moist receptive earth. The foolishness of spring's mating appears with the third charm.

SACRED MARRIAGES

Three for a Wedding

Spring's adolescents have matured with the calendar's passage of time. Having been initiated, purified, and prepared for their coming role in the fertility of Earth, in the farming world, the land is ready for plowing. Lightning's arrows seed new life in Earth's moist furrows.

Time's turning wheel brings us to the third month of March, ruled by arrow-shooting Mars ♂: "The world was created on the 25th of March, which made the world to begin on that day."[3] We have arrived

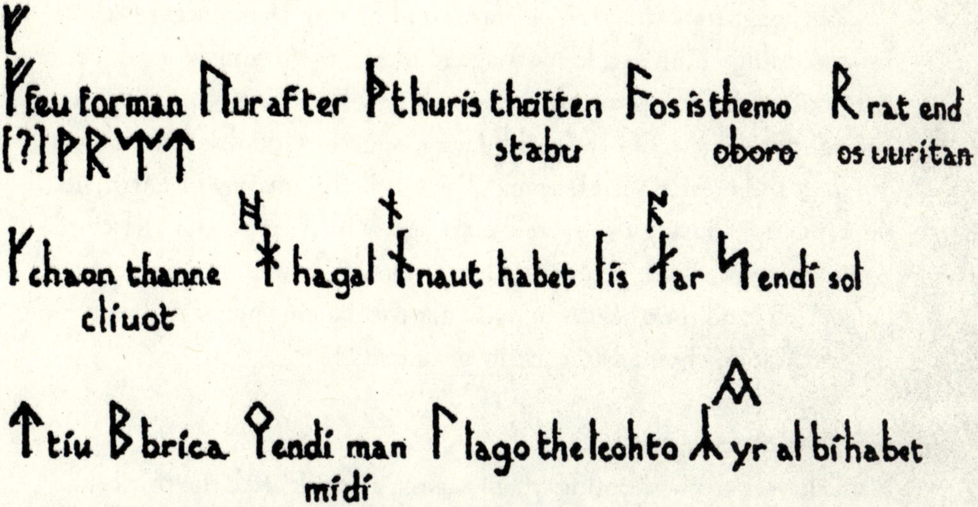

feu forman ur after thuris thriten stabu os is themo oboro rat end os uuritan
[?]
chaon thanne cliuot hagal naut habet is ar endi sol
tiu brica endi man midi lago the leohto yr al bihabet

Fig. 6. A version of the Younger Futhark, *Abecedarium Nordmannicum*, c. 825 CE. Reproduced from R. Derolez, *Runica Manuscripta*, 78. Original from 1828 copy by Wilhelm Grimm.

at the Spring Equinox, the day the sacred marriage between the king and his land was celebrated in the ancient world.

In our oldest known rune poem, the *Abecedarium Nordmannicum* (circa 825 CE),* under Fehu's promise of wealth, the runes spell out Tir and Earth. Tir, or Tues, ↑ is an ancient arrow god who is identified with Mars and who gave his name to Tuesday, our third day. Because God stated, "It was good" twice on the third day of Genesis, Judaism sees this day as the best one for a wedding, and the line from children's nursery rhyme below agrees:

One for sorrow,
Two for mirth,
Three for a wedding,
And four for a birth

MOTHER GOOSE NURSERY RHYME

*Found in the *Codex Sangallensis 878*, which is kept in the Abbey of St. Gall in Switzerland.

The magnetic attraction of heaven and earth is the subject of "three for a wedding." This sacred marriage results in the drying of a woman's red flood while her womb thickens with new life. We have reached the Drought of March. On the third day of Genesis, God dried the waters of Earth and created seed-bearing plants. It is this seeding of Earth, her impregnation during the sacred marriage, which empowers the third symbol's magic. With pregnancy, her waters are bound, her red seas no longer flow, and time begins to mark out the dancing hours. Still counting out a clock's hours is the arrow of Mars (Tir).

Horse-Headed Mars

Named after arrow-shooting Mars, March, a "prick" like the third rune Thurisaz (thorn), also translates as both "border" and "horse." Horse-headed Mars rules red-rusting iron, which connects him with the secrets of metallurgy begged, borrowed, or stolen along with the magic of fertility. Iron "is one of only three naturally occurring magnetic elements [. . .] the other two are nickel and cobalt," and iron is found in both the earth and in blood. It is the property of an object that spells its use as a symbol.

An important part of northern spring rituals, "horse fights remained popular in Scandinavia well into Christian times. They were

Fig. 7. Circa 500 CE, Haggeby, Sweden.

Drawing by CF Dillon after Haggeby picture stone.

held in spring in Norway and were believed to ensure good crops."[4] The winning stallion may have been ultimately sacrificed—"Mars was the only god to whom a horse was sacrificed"[5]—but first he covered a herd of mares. Among Christians, March 25 became Lady Day, the day that Mary learned she carried a baby.

ARROW-SHOOTING GIANTS AND PREGNANCY

Giant (Þurs) causes anguish to women; misfortune makes few men cheerful.

OLD NORWEGIAN RUNE POEM

While women desired children, it was a dangerous time in their lives. Many did not survive childbirth.

Giant (Þurs) is the torment of women and the dweller in the rocks and the husband of Vardh-runa.

Þurs er kvenna kvöl ok kletta búi ok varðrúnar verr. Saturnus þengill.
Glosses: *Saturnus* (Saturn) *and þengil* (king)

OLD ICELANDIC RUNE POEM, THORSSON TRANS.

Skadi/Var, the Bride of Scandinavia mentioned earlier, is described as a *jotunn* (giant) and a "fair maiden." Her first husband was the earth god Njord, identified with Saturn, one of the (many) names for the stars of giant Orion.[6] Ruler of a lost Golden Age, Saturn was once the lord of seeds and wealth. Orion, like Tir and Mars, is identified as an arrow-shooting giant, although some cultures saw him simply as an arrow.

After leaving her first husband, Skadi returned to her frozen mountains to marry one-eyed Odin. Since kings needed to marry the bride of the land, he was "Skadi's mate in [Sweden], and the fell-sliding

Ski-goddess begot with Odin many sons."[7] In our era, Skadi is one of planet Saturn's moons, and her father, Thiazzi, whose two eyes were tossed up into heaven, names another of Saturn's moons.

Drought of March and Bonds of Time

> *The third I chant thee: If great waters threaten to overwhelm thee, may flood and foam turn back to Hell the while, and dry up before thee.*
>
> "SVIPDAGSMAL," VIGFUSSON AND POWELL TRANS.

Once Lady Earth's fertile crescent is impregnated, her flowing waters are bound until delivery at the fourth charm. The goddess Groa (growing), chanting charms from her grave, teaches her son the magic of binding red floods with the spell above.

At the foot of one of the World Tree's three great root in the cold, moist world of Hel, lies the well Hvergelmir (bubbling spring), the source of the northern rivers. They were created by a stag: "There is a stag named Eikthyrnir who stands on Odin's Hall and gnaws the limbs of the tree Laerath. Drops fall from his horns into the well of Hvergelmir; that is the origin of all the rivers."[8] Groa's charm returns all waters back to their origins here in Hel's womb.

Knots and Bindings

Through seeding and impregnation, Time and Death enter a now martial world of war and triangular arrow heads, along with the bonds of Time. In the Chinese tradition, the third mythic emperor introduced time, acupuncture, knots, and the instruments of war. The Third Hall of Asgaard belongs to Odin, owner of a magic knot of binding: "A third home is there [. . .] Valaskjolf [Shelf of the Dead] is it, in days of old set by a god for himself."[9]

The valknut (the triple knot) had Odin's power to bind and unbind. With it, he "could make his enemies in battle blind, or deaf, or terror-struck, and their weapons so blunt that they could no more but than a willow wand."[10] Odin claimed, "I know a third spell: If I have a great need to thwart my enemies, I dull the edges of their weapons, and none of their blades will bite."[11]

Three has other associations with impregnation and bonds. Although I have been concentrating on the fertility aspects of the third charm, the knots and bonds may also have been used to prevent pregnancy. Women in the ancient world knew ways to control the number of their children: "Possibly knotting of cords played a part in contraception as it did in healing or the more notorious intervention of impotence magic."[12]

It is interesting to note that a woman is most likely to become pregnant during three specific days of her menstrual cycle: the two days before and the day of ovulation. Binding her legs together on those days greatly reduces conception. For those desiring a full womb, the three days offer the greatest chance.

Now that the womb of pregnant Earth has been bound, the knot magic of this charm must be loosened to enable waters of delivery to flow with the fourth charm.

4. Ansus or Oss

High God or Mouth (ᚫ)

Out of the One comes Two, out of Two comes Three, and from the Third comes the One as the Fourth.

Mark Haeffner, *The Dictionary of Alchemy*

DELIVERY OF WORDS AND WORLDS

Mouth (Os) is the source of all language, a pillar of wisdom and a comfort to wise man, a blessing and a joy to every knight.

Old English Rune Poem

Oss (mouth), or Ass (God), is the fourth rune. Although gods eventually took over the mother's delta to speak words and worlds into existence, Ass is "long been thought to be related to $h_2$ens—'to engender' (cf. Hittite hass—to procreate, give birth')"[1] That is, the Ass and her delta once wore a very real female aspect. The name of our fourth month, April, may derive from *aperire* meaning "to open." The drought of March is now at an end. The waters of birth now flow with the April showers as the bonds are loosened.

The fourth Phoenician letter (Dalet) ◁ is the "door" through which we now begin our journey into the material world. Among

Fig. 8. Egypt's Delta.
Courtesy of NASA.

the runes, this door is an estuary (Oss), which is "the way of most journeys."* An estuary is the meeting of the river's arrow with the mothering sea (Mare). Here, the very female delta forms as new earth is birthed at the watery mouth (Oss) of the river. As the river sheaths itself in the sea, the rune poem ends with the scabbard sheathing the sword.

The magic of the fourth charm loosens the womb bound by the third, permitting new life to emerge through the delta of our letter D† Ancient goddesses understood the powers of untangling knots binding a woman's womb. Juno, the Roman goddess of childbirth, permitted no

*Old Norwegian Rune Poem.

†Myth is amazingly consistent. The Bible Study website states: "God overcame the [. . .] rebellious humans when he [flooded] the earth on the 17th of the second Hebrew month." The first Hebrew month, Nisan, falls around the March equinox, and second Hebrew month, Iyar, falls between April and May, our fourth month's April showers.

knots in her temples, which were thought to impede the delivery of the baby. April Showers now end the Drought of March.

LORE AND TRADITION

The warrior Odin adapting the birth magic sang, "I know a fourth spell; if chains and locks are placed upon my limbs, I cast this spell so that I can escape. The chains burst from my hands; the locks burst from my feet."[2] The spell was so widely known that the British historian, the Venerable Bede (d. 735), described a young Northumbrian prisoner who was shackled each night to prevent his escape. Each morning his shackles had fallen off, and he was asked if he had any hidden "loosening letters,"[3] meaning runes.

> *Óss (God) is aged Gaultr [Goth] and prince of Asgardr and lord of Valhalla.*
>
> *Óss er algingautr ok ásgarðs jöfurr, ok valhallar vísi. Jupiter oddviti.*
> Glosses: Jupiter, *oddviti* (leader)
>
> Old Icelandic Rune Poem

King Jupiter assumed four's square throne. Odin, lord of Valhalla, is glossed as Jupiter in the OIRP. Jupiter's symbol, used by NASA, is our numeral four: ♃ In alchemy, this symbol represents tin. Originally an Etruscan sky god, like Jupiter and other Asses and emperors residing among the fourth symbols, Tin was a king. Tin married Copper (Venus) to produce the brass and bronze used for a warrior's sword. Because this position concerns the charms of speaking new worlds into life, sweet sounding bells and singing bowls are produced from brass.* Jupiter (and King Tin) both spoke with the sound of thunder.

With the fourth charm, the One as ruler is born. In the creation

*While modern brass is a zinc/copper alloy, brass made with tin is resistant to salt water corrosion, useful for ocean travelling northmen.

story of Genesis, on the fourth day, the sun and moon are created to rule the sky. Odin (Woden), naming the fourth day of the week, Wednesday, shares his watery home in the Fourth Hall of April showers with Saga: "Sokkvabekk (Sinking Stream) is the fourth, where cool waves flow, and amid their murmur it stands; There daily do Othin and Saga drink in gladness from cups of gold."[4]

Not much is known about the goddess Saga, but "the name suggests some relation to history or storytelling." While earlier earth goddesses gave birth through their deltas, later gods spoke worlds into being, and the word was made flesh.

The speaking of laws at the yearly assembly begins on our fifth day with the fifth rune: "Runes of Speech (Mal-runar) thou must know [. . .] when the assembly is going into full court."[5]

5. Raido

Journey

Variants: Rad or Reið

Wheel or ride (ᚱ)

Riding (Rad) seems easy to every warrior while he is indoors and very courageous to him who traverses the high roads on the back of a stout horse.

Old English Rune Poem

THE RADIATION OF WISDOM

We now arrive at the perfect fifth, the pure quintessence. Once the square foundation of four becomes five, the radiation around a centering pupil becomes possible. Eye magic is one of the attributes empowering rune spells attributed to the number five: "I know a fifth spell: If I see a spear cast into a crowd of battling foes, it cannot fly so fast that I can't change its course, as long as I can see it."[1]

Voice of the Wind

Rad at the end is written mouth.

Abecedarium Nordmannicum

The breathy wind of the fifth Phoenician letter, Hey, 𐤄 has also been translated as "window" from the Anglo-Saxon *vindr*, meaning the "wind's eye." When Hebrew changed the shapes of their alphabet from Old Hebrew/Phoenician to modern Hebrew, they added a window to Hey, ה, letting the speaking wind pass through.

RITUAL PURITY

"In Indo-European languages the first four numerals were declined, with feminine and masculine forms. Five is not declined, having only one form."[2] The nonsexual quintessence is the purest, most perfect manifestation of a being. As such, there is a celibacy associated with the fifth charm: "I counsel thee fifthly: Though thou seest fair brides on the bench, let them not hinder thy sleep. Do not allure women to kisses."[3]

Travel and the Gift of Law

> *Riding (Reið) joy of the horsemen and speedy journey and toil of the steed.*
>
> *Reið er sitjandi sæla ok snúðig ferð ok jórs erfiði. iter ræsir.*
> Glosses: *Iter* (journey) and *ræsir* (chief or king)
>
> Old Icelandic Rune Poem

Three's bonds have been loosened by the fourth charm; we are free to journey forth. In the North, freed from the icy spring of Var (Skadi), summer began on the fifth day of Thursday.[4] May, our warm fifth month, was the time to ride forth, to radiate: During "Whitsuntide [. . .] Pentecost (fiftieth day) [. . .] Knights from King Arthur's court set off to begin the great Quests."[5]

In addition to travel, there is a transmission of laws and wisdom within the radiant circle of the fifth charm. Among Jews, the celebration of the receiving of the Five Books of Law (Torah) during this season mandated a pilgrimage to the Temple of Jerusalem before its destruction. People gathered to share the harvest of the season and to receive the Law. In Iceland, people made the journey each summer to hear laws proclaimed. Iceland, like Ireland, was divided into four provinces with the council as the (fifth) mystical center.

"Rad id est consilium."[6] The definition of consilium includes counsel, council, and wisdom. According to Snorri Sturluson "Wisdom is called sagacity; counsel, understanding."[7]

THE CYCLE OF VENUS

The cycles of the planet Venus pace out the five-pointed star still worn by marshals of the law. Venus has five morning risings, and each time she rises, she appears in a different zodiac sign.

The numbers five and eight are associated with Venus's path through the sky. She travels 1.6 years between each heliacal (morning) rising. The entire cycle returning her to the original zodiac position takes 8 years (8/1.6 = 5), and each appearance in a different zodiac sign traces out that five-pointed star in the sky (360/5 = 72). Each arc contains the important number 72 degrees: the slow backward movement of the stars during the precession of the equinoxes is one degree every 72 years.

RIDDLES, THUMBS, AND SPEAKING IN TONGUES

> *The most important finger is the thumb, which among other things, is strong in virtue and power.*
>
> T. H. WHITE, *THE BOOK OF BEASTS*

In the magic of this radiating season, four fingers circle around the thumb, the fifth finger. The giant thumb's association with the number five suggests the naming of the fifth day, Thursday, after Thor, who is identified with both with the red giant Jupiter and Hercules. In palmistry, the thumb is given to the rule of Hercules.

According to Herodotus (Book IV), "From Scythes, the son of

Hercules, were descended the after kings of the Scythians."[8] They were the wild Indo Europeans travelling in wagons and by horse between Mongolia and the Black Sea. Like the Vanir who taught the art of far-seeing to the northern gods, and like the Norse use of rune staves, they threw staves to divine knowledge.

While neither giant Thor nor his priests were celibate like other deities associated with this position, Thursday was the northern day to deliver law: "It is significant that the Althing, the Law Assembly of heathen Iceland, opened on a Thursday, the day of Thor."[9] In India, another culture adapting the ancient number magic, law in their villages is distributed by a group of five elders (*panchayat raj*).

Dragon Blood and Thumb Magic

> *Sigurd gave the serpent wounds.*
>
> *Edda*, Anthony Faulkes trans.

> *Riding (Ræið) is said to be the worst thing for horses.*
> *Reginn forged the finest sword.*
>
> Old Norwegian Rune Poem

The following Norse myth refers to Five's thumb magic and the gift of tongues, which for Christians happened at Pentecost (fiftieth day). After killing the great serpent-dragon Fafnir with a sword forged by the smith Regin, Sigurd roasted the dragon's heart. In the process, he got a drop of the dragon's blood on his thumb, which he popped into his mouth. This taste of dragon blood gave him the ability to understand the speech of birds. After hearing them discussing Regin's plan to kill him, he murdered Regin and then went on to claim the dragon's gold:

> Then Sigurdr went over to Reginn and slew him, and thence to his horse, which was named Grani, and rode till he came to Fáfnir's lair. He took up the gold, trussed it up in his saddlebags, laid it upon Grani's back, mounted up himself, and then rode his ways.[10]

Fig. 9. Drawing of Ramsund carving depicting Sigurd's heroic feats, circa 1030 BCE.

Courtesy of *Nordisk familjebok*.

Grani, Sigurd's horse, is descended from Odin's eight-legged steed who could travel between the realms. Allusions to Sigurd and the dragon's cursed gold appear frequently among the existing rune poems. As the reader will find, everyone who owns it eventually dies.

In the image above, Sigurd sucks his blood-covered thumb (labeled 1), and Grani is ready to carry off the gold. Decapitated Regin (left; labeled 3) lies by the sword. Myth meeting history, Fafnir's lair of Gnitaheidr is today known as Bad Salzuflen, an area famous for the fire-breathing dragon's legacy: thermal hot springs.

Shield Magic

> The Fifth Hall of the gods is Gladés-heimr (Place of Joy) and gold-bright where stands Valhalla stretching wide: There the Sage (Woden) chooses everyday weapon-dead men. That hall is very easy to know for all that come to visit Woden; the house is raftered with shafts, the hall is thatched with shields, the benches are strewn with mail-coats [. . .] A wolf hangs before the west door, an eagle hovers above it.[11]

Fig. 10. Shield maiden, Galgebakken in Denmark, five circles appear on her shield.

Photo by Jon Lee, National Museum of Denmark

The Fifth Hall belonging to Odin does not seem to fit the usual attributes of the fifth symbol unless it is the reference to the shields. Among the dead warriors revived to fight each day in Valhalla until their final battle on the Day of the Wolf, Odin's shield maidens (Valkyries) are also present. Many protective shields were associated with the number five. Homer describes the smith Hephaestus making Achilles a shield made of five folds of metal and illustrating it with the sky.

6. Ken or Kaun

Torch or Ulcer (ᚴ)

Variants: Kenaz, Cen, Kano (ᚲ)

Torch (Cen) is known to every living man by its pale, bright flame; it always burns where princes sit within.

OLD ENGLISH RUNE POEM

Five for silver, Six for gold

MOTHER GOOSE NURSERY RHYME

BRIDE OF THE LAND

Thrymheim the sixth is called where Þjazi lived, the all-powerful giant; but now Skadi, the shining bride of the gods, lives in her father's ancient courts.

"GRIMNISMAL,"
CAROLYNE LARRINGTON TRANS.

While *ken* means to know one in the biblical sense, it is also one of the names given the shining sixth rune (Kenaz or Cen). The sixth charm belongs to the maturing Bride of the Land. No longer a princess, she is a queen who now assumes her glorious role in midsummer's marriage.

The bright honeymoon of June's sixth month is named after Juno, protector goddess of Roman lands. Friday, our sixth day, is named after earthy Freya. This is the night the Sabbath bride joins her Israel. In Spanish, the sixth day is *viernes* after lovely Venus. These fertile goddesses produce summer's golden wealth; red roses once decorated their marriage beds.

Six is sex

BARBARA WALKER,
WOMAN'S DICTIONARY

In the midsummer festivals, the land is again seeded to ensure her delivery of summer's gold. Jumping over torch-kindled fires lit this season was a country way to bring luck and to secure a marriage. A traditional rhyme tells us: "Jack be nimble, Jack be quick. Jack jump over the candlestick." *Kindle*, according to the dictionary, is from Old Norse *kynda*, influenced by Old Norse *kindill*, meaning "candle" or "torch": the sixth rune.

Mother Goose, another name for the ancient goddess, leaves us yet more gifts here. She sang, "Five for silver, six for gold": the silver-tongued devil is the speaking wind of the fifth symbol, and summer-seeded grain is the gold of the sixth. Jack was associated with country folk who kept the old ways. While Jack is a knave, a fool, a simpleton, and a jack-of-all-trades, he is also the one-eyed fool, the Jack of Hearts who stole the Queen of Heaven's cakes (baked all on a summer day).

Fig. 11. One-eyed Jack of Hearts.

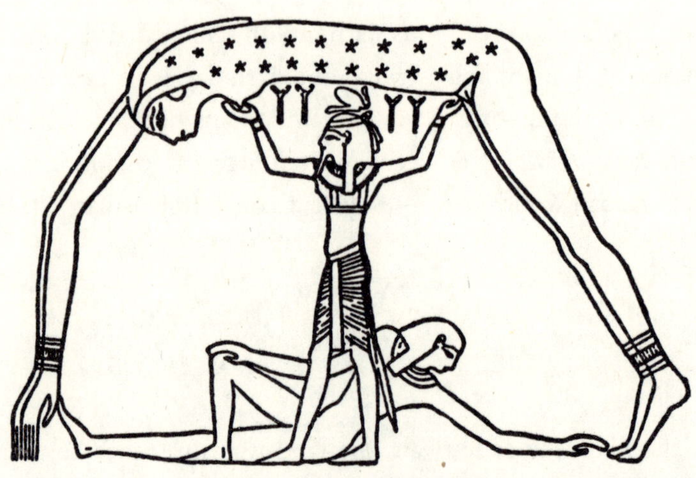

Fig. 12. Egyptian drawing

From Louis Herbert Gray. *The Mythology of All Races*. Marshall Jones Company (1918), 44.

In the Egyptian image above, Earth and Sky mate to produce their young. Separated by air so other children could be born, *Y*-shaped hooks hold Sky in place.

Languages and alphabet letters contain the shadows of their forgotten ancestors. The sixth Phoenician letter (Wau), *Y*-shaped like the hooks holding up Egypt's sky, is translated as "hook" or "nail." In Hebrew, the letter is known as the "vav" of connection because it represents "and," the joining together of people and objects. The *Y*-shape in Old Teutonic, thought to be a form of the knotty Thurisaz (thorn) rune, has the dictionary meaning of "with" and "together" (a joining) when used as a prefix.

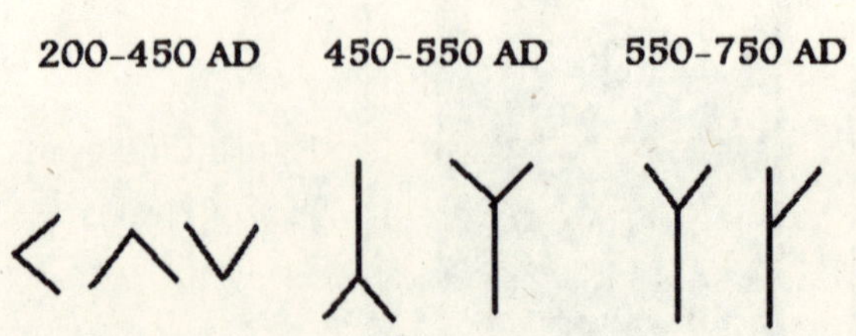

Fig. 13. Different shapes of Kenaz rune, including the Y shape originally used for Phoenician's "hook" (wau).

Image Credit: Berig (2009).

Other traditions marry their symbols in a more abstract way. A six-pointed star mates the fiery male spirit with the female matter ✡. Like other sixth symbols, the upward thrusting male triangle joins the female delta. Similar in concept, the sixth letter of ancient Greek is a digamma, two gammas (Γ+ Γ) joined to create our sixth letter *F.*

MIDSUMMER MARRIAGES

The bride and her dark lover, first joined in spring, now prepare for their summer wedding. At the sun's peak on the summer solstice, they again exchange marriage vows. In the North, power belonged to the Queen of the Land, so kings had to marry the land if they wish to rule: "The pine-haired deserted wife of Third [Odin]; his deserted wife is [Skadi, the land of Norway]."[1] A king must sweetly mount her throne, sit on her lap, and enter her house to attain legitimate rule for his children. Mother Nature accepted all her children as legitimate, so it was probably a concern with paternity that demanded later kings legally marry their land.

Skadi's marriage to a Vanir came about through the death of her father, the frost giant Þjazi. He was traveling as an eagle when the trickster god Loki struck him with a stick which stuck. The giant refused to let Loki go unless he captured Idunn, the wife of Braggi, the god of poetry, along with her apples of youth. Braggi was Odin's child with Gunlodd, keeper of the mead stolen by Odin. Forced to retrieve Idunn, Loki changed her into a nut, shapeshifted into a falcon, and was flying home when Þjazi pursued him in his eagle shape. The Aesir built a huge fire, and unable to stop in time, Þjazi flying as the eagle died in the flames.

When Skadi arrived to kill her father's assassins, they placated her by offering her marriage to the Vanir Njord. It was not a happy marriage. They shared nine nights each in Skadi's icy home among the wolves, alternating with Njord's home by the sea. Disturbed by the screeching gulls, Skadi returned home, and their marriage ended.

Kings wed the Brides of the Land in various northern kingdoms. For instance, Thorgerdr, an earth goddess, is the bride of Helgi, founder of Halogaland, an area of Norway. Her name has been associated with the jotunn (giant) Gerd, bride of Yngvi-Freyr, the ancestors of the dynasty of Ynglings.

Skadi, as we've seen, is the shadow Bride of Norway, who married Odin, along with many others, and gave him children:

To Asa's son Queen Skade bore Saeming,
who dyed his shield in gore,
The iron pine-tree's daughter, she
To Odin bore full many a son,
Heroes of many a battle won.

"The Ynglinga Saga," in *The Heimskrilinga Saga*,
Samuel Laing trans.

Kings of the North

Midsummer's wedding and mating produced the kin of each new generation and resulted in the families of the kings of the land. After leaving Asia, Odin "went into the north, until he was stopped by the sea, which men thought lay around all the lands of the earth; and there he set his son over this kingdom, which is now called Norway. This king was Sæmingr; the kings of Norway trace their lineage from him."[2] As in the above poem, Skade bore him.

Heimdall, the Watcher of the Gods, once left his rainbow bridge to assume the name Rig (king) and fathered each class of people. The youngest of his three sons, Kon, a golden young prince, engenders the line of new kings. Like all mortal kings, in time he, too, must eventually pass his torch.

Venus and the Fall toward Death

Ulcer (Kaun) disease fatal to children and painful spot and abode of mortification.

Kaun er barna böl ok bardaga [för] ok holdfúa hús.
flagella konungr.
Glosses: *Flagella* (whip) and *konungr* (young king)

Old Icelandic Rune Poem

Ulcer (Kaun) is fatal to children; death makes a corpse pale.
OLD NORWEGIAN RUNE POEM

Venus of many names was one aspect of the summertime Queen. By the time the later rune poems were written, Kenaz, the rune belonging to lovely Venus, became Kaun representing venereal sores. Venus's dancing hours, no longer horis, had become whores. The gloss *flagella* (whip) on the OIRP does not seem to fit the usual attributes of number six but here may relate to Kaun's venereal "ulcer" or to the old tradition of beating fruit trees to make them produce. The gloss *konungr* is the "young king" produced by mating.

By the time this rune poem was written down, the earlier joy of seed-begetting pregnancy and childbirth had been replaced by a curse. Our third finger, Saturn's finger in palmistry, represents both a curse and the f*cking finger, illustrated by folding down all other fingers to denote, "Go screw." Roses once decorating Venus's honeymoon bed had become a ring-around-the rosy of plague, and her gay gold ring with which kings once courted, became a cankerous thing.

Such changes are reflected in the sun's seasonal journey. When it reaches the gate of Cancer, the stars of the midsummer season, the sun reverses, dying south toward winter. Despite the later overlay of horror, the old pleasures were never quite forgotten. Lovers still meet for their Friday night date and spoon beneath June's honeymoon. But at the end of Midsummer's golden honeymoon, both honeybee king and Sun begin losing strength, dying south. The prime of the longest day passes as the Sun moves toward his fall, but Earth never dies. She stores the seed of each dying king until he returns as another year.

The Spirit of Fountain dies not. It is called the Mysterious Feminine.
LAOZI, *TAO TE CHING*, JOHN WU TRANS., VERSE 6*

*Not further explored in this paper, the Tao is another earthy alchemical tradition following the alphabet pattern.

7. Gyfu

Gift

Variant: Gebo

Gyfu brings credit and honour, which support one's dignity; it furnishes help and subsistence to all broken men who are devoid of aught else.

Old English Rune Poem

Hey the Gift, ho the Gift. Hey the Gift on the living, Son of the dawn, Son of the clouds, Son of the planet, Son of the star.

Alexander Carmichael,
Celtic Prayers and Incantations

CROSSING THE BORDERLANDS

As in all earth magic, help and subsistence are promised as we cross each border. The X shape of the Gyfu rune imitates the shape of Phoenicia's last letter, Tau. It is written as an *X*, *T*, or +. Multiplication and plus signs promise an increase or a good return wherever they appear.

T, Tav or Tau

In the circling Mysteries of Hebrew, when the last letter *T* is reached, one returns to A. Tau/Tav, translated as "mark," is significant to many traditions. God put a mark on Cain to save him from death. The mark painted on doorposts saved enslaved Jews from plagues killing the first-born of Egypt. In the Mysteries of wine, *marc* is the residue after the grapes have been trampled underfoot. The earliest known vineyards were in Anatolia, near Lake Van where a drunken Noah landed his ark after the flood. This is where Odin learned his runes and drank his share of the wine: "The weapon-blessed Odin lives on wine alone."[1] And in Buddhism, the Sanskrit word *marg*, meaning "path" or "way," is the guide of footprints the returning soul must follow.

Following the Footprints

At seven's charm, the physical body is abandoned. When the aging king leaves his earthly home, when he steps off the world, he leaves his "mark" behind, the sole-print his prince must emulate as he follows in his father's footsteps.

There are multitudes of prints left where gods, saints, kings, or buddhas stepped off the earth, leaving behind their pledge. Scythians, kin to the Celts and Northmen, have a famous footprint pressed into a rock in Tyras: "The country [Scythia] has no marvels except its rivers [. . .] and one thing besides, which I am about to mention. They show a footmark of Hercules, impressed on a rock, in the shape like a man's foot, but two cubits in length. It is in the neighborhood of the Tyras."[2] Tyras was a city founded by colonists from Miletus near the early Turkish home of the Aesir and Vanir gods. Miletus claimed Cadmus as their founder, and his grandson, leaving his "marc" behind, was the wine-mad Dionysius.

The footprints of buddhas are meant to remind Buddhists that Buddha was present on earth and left a spiritual marg, or path, to be followed. In other traditions, these footprints might also promise a safe return: "Romans were accustomed to carve pairs of footprints on a stone with the inscription *pro itu et reditu*, 'the journey and return.' They used them for protective rites on leaving for a journey and for thanksgiving for a safe return."[3]

The more literal Germans swore binding oaths upon their "soles:"

Fig. 14. Gunnar playing harp in snake pit, Hylestad stave church, Norway.
Photo by Fabullus.

"On entering upon a league, the ancients were wont to soak their footprints with a mutual aspersion of gore, that their pledges of friendliness might be established by the blending of their blood."[4] A "league" is a covenant, a pledge between people. It also measures the path they walk together. The oath upon their soles was sworn by Sigurd and his brother-in-law Gunnar before Gunnar betrayed him.

The broken pledge linked to the story of the cursed Rhine gold. The oath breaker Gunnar caused Sigurd's death which ultimately led to his own death. The Niebeling Gunnar, the last living person to know the location of the gold, dies in a snake pit after refusing to reveal its location to his sister's last husband, Attila the Hun.

Cross My Heart

The ale runes rely on the Gyfu rune's protective cross (X) to protect drinkers from poison or murder: "Ale runes (Al-runar) thou must know [. . .] Cross thy cup against ill; and throw leak [leek] into the liquor, then I know that thy mead will never be poisoned."[5]

Vikings took their drinking (and another's wife if they were strong enough) very seriously. Drinking in the Frisian (Dutch) way became a symbol of excess, but drinking a comrade under the table once marked male prowess rather than dissolution. Alcohol gave one "Dutch courage" and strength, and a "Dutch treat" implies each person contributed his "gift" (Gyfu).

But drinking could also be a dangerous activity. To refuse a drink was a deadly insult settled by knife or fist. To accept the drink could be equally lethal as the ale might be poisoned by any number of substances. The act of raising the cup to swallow exposed one's throat to an enemy, and attendance at a banquet, lulled by food and drink, might end with the doors being barred and the building burned. Sigrdrifa, awakened from her sleep by the dragon slayer Sigurd advises him: "I counsel thee seventhly: If thou hast to fight out a quarrel with dauntless men, better to fight than be burnt in the house."[6]

What to do? What to do? Happily, the custom of pledging, the crossing one's heart, evolved and became a necessary part of what was becoming an increasingly dangerous social life. When someone pledged another drinker's health, he crossed his heart and then stood guard while the drinker safely finished his drink. The first drinker then guarded the second. Note that a double cross negated the pledge. Pledges eventually included both friendship and romantic love. The woman was allowed to kiss the glass (or her lover) without drinking.

THE COMING DELUGE

Only the Old English Rune Poem includes the Elder Futhark's seventh rune. Others have dropped Gyfu from their letters. In many traditions, seven is the number of endings. Destruction by fire and water arrive with the seventh symbol. A coming Deluge may empower this seventh spell to put out fires: "I know a seventh spell if I see a great flame consuming a hall full of people, it cannot burn so bright that I cannot save those inside; I know how to cast this spell."[7]

Continuing the association with water, the seventh day, Saturday, is washing day in the Viking world: In Scandinavian countries, Saturday is called *lördag*, The name is derived from laugardagr—a compound of *laug* ("bath") + *dagr* ("day")—literally meaning "bath day." This is due to the northern practice of bathing on Saturdays.[8]

Saturday is named after aging Saturn, the "Lord of the Rings" whose name is literally "seven." Some of his avatars are Osiris of Egypt and giant Orion. In one myth, Isis, as the star Sirius, follows her brother Osiris as Orion, crying tears over his death. Her tears flood the waters of the Nile when her star rises in our seventh month of July.

Another group of stars associated with seven's rising waters are the Pleiades. Out of the seven stars in the cluster only six are now seen by the naked eye. Some myths describe the loss of the seventh Pleiad by saying she ran away to marry one of the polestars.

In the calendars of Mesoamerica, every 52 years the ceremony to mark the end of time coincided with a precise observation of the Pleiades at midnight, when it appeared exactly upon the meridian. The Earth-Pleiades conjunction was held to be of such importance to the Maya and the Aztecs that they believed it might mark the end of the world. To prevent this, a human sacrifice occurred when the Pleiades culminated at end of the 52-year cycle.[9]

NUMBER MAGIC

Number magic is widespread and ancient. Our Western tradition lays out 52 weeks of 7 days in a 364-day year. Common decks of playing cards also number 52. Coming from China via India, Persia, and Egypt, they begin with the "ace," highest or lowest number of a deck that contains the astronomically important number of 13 cards in each of the four suits. The ace is the one-eyed, snake-eye roll of a die (plural is dice). Dice herself is one of the dark Fate goddesses. "Dice was in charge of justice [. . .] she not only punished injustice but rewarded virtue."*[10]

Now facing death, and endings, seventh Phoenician letter is "weapon" (Zain). Among the cards, the King of Diamonds is typically shown with an axe behind his head with the blade facing toward him. The King of Hearts is threatened by his sword. These depictions, and their blood-red color, inspired the nickname "suicide kings." King cards have a value of 13. The sharp axe returns us to the fierce form of the Pleiades and the letter weapon of Zain.

*Note: While I am suspicious of strange connections, the sum of 52 is seven (5 + 2 = 7).

Fig. 15. Aluette card deck.
B. P. Grimaud editor, France, 1858–1890.

India, another culture inheriting the number magic underlying the runic pattern, measures her lunar calendar by 28 mansions. The moon passes through the homes of his 28 wives on his round through the month. Over a year, he has visited each wife 13 times. The mansion of the Pleiades is Krittika, meaning knife or "cutter," a sharp object like weapon as seventh Phoenician letter; like the axe and sword threatening the Suicide Kings. The northern tradition of begins winter on Saturday (seven); winter arrives in India when the moon enters the Pleiades' house of Kartika.

DEATH AND RESURRECTION

Balder, best-loved of Odin's sons, lived in the Seventh Hall of the gods:

> *Broad-blink is the seventh, there Balder has made him a hall; the land in which the fewest curses lie [the most blessed of lands.]*
>
> "Grimnismal," Vigfusson and Powell trans.

After an arrow of mistletoe killed white, shining Balder, his death began the chain of events leading to the destruction of the gods at Ragnarok, when gods, monsters, and giants make war: "The sun turns black, land sinks into the sea, the bright stars vanish from the sky; steam rises up in the conflagration, hot flame plays high against heaven itself." Seas will rise, and a great Deluge will cover the land, putting out the fires of war. After the death of the gods, Balder will be reborn into the new green world: "Without sowing, the fields will grow, all evil will be healed. Baldr will come."[11]

Seven's Celebrations and Symbols

Dark Nemesis, the hag mother of Apollo and Artemis, celebrated her holidays on the seventh of the month. Her son Apollo is the only other Greek god to celebrate on the seventh: "All Apollo's festivals were celebrated on the seventh day of the month; the other Greek gods choosing the full moon for their worship."[12]

The Hags and Crones of the dying year are included among seven's symbols. Delivering the kiss of death,* the soul fleeing its worn host was gathered into a womb to wait rebirth into another circle. Earth, taking the seed of kings into her generous womb, now ages into a winter Hag, but like her dying king she will be renewed as a virgin spring.

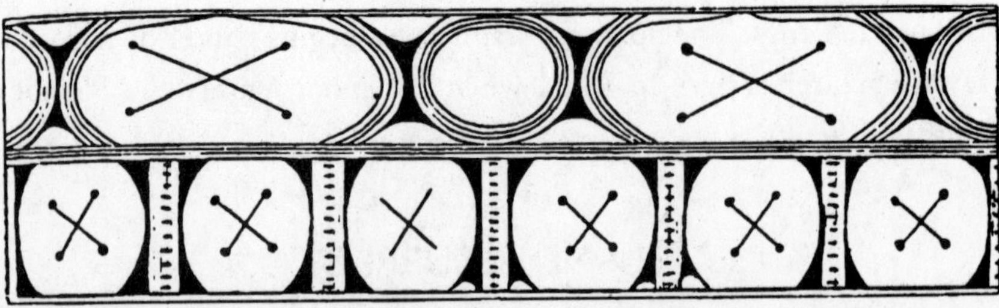

Fig. 16. Sipenitsi pattern, Ukraine, c. 3800 BCE.
From Gimbutas, *The Language of the Goddess*, 218.

*It's interesting to note that kisses are written as X's and hugs as 0's. Osculate: To kiss. In mathematics, means to have contact with a higher order.

8. Wunjo or Wynn

Joy or White

The eighth I sing is for everyone the most fortunate lore he can learn: When hatred is harbored by children of chiefs, this I can hastily heal.

Elsa-Brita Titchenell, *The Masks of Odin*

Wynne (Joy) is had by the one who knows few troubles pains, and sorrows, and to him who himself has power and blessedness, and a good enough house.

Old English Rune Poem, Thorsson trans.

THE WINSOME JOY OF THE SUMMER HARVEST

Our calendar month now brings us into late August, a harvest month. Here we find storehouses where the ancient goddess kept the harvest until needed. Although the Norse stories do not seem to describe the earth goddesses as bottomless pits, the concept helps understand eight's symbol.

The eighth Phoenician letter Heth (gate or fence) 𐤇 reflects the shape depicted on the womb of the Anatolian goddess pictured on the next page and the gate through which harvested kings and their seed are carried. The children of Heth provided the cave to biblical Abraham

Fig. 17. Goddess figure, Anatolia, c. 2500 BCE. Gimbutas, *The Language of the Goddess*, 11.

for his burial. We will meet the northern goddess of the underworld tomb at the ninth rune.

Eventually the gate to earth's treasures moved to heaven, and its symbol became a symbol for Hel's ninth rune. Note that Hekate, the Underworld goddess of witches from Anatolia, is another "gate" at the liminal crossroads of time and place. If encountering her, you'd be wise to employ the eighth charm: "The eighth I chant thee: If the night overtake thee on a path of darkness, may the [evil] night-riding witches have no power to come and harm thee."[1]

Venus and Virgo

When we follow the soul's path through the eighth position, number eight belongs to winsome Venus. Joy and white, meanings of the eighth rune Wunjo, or Wynn, are names associated with Venus.

Venus embodies sex, beauty, enticement, seduction, and persuasive female charm among the community of immortal gods. In Latin orthography, her name is indistinguishable from the Latin noun *venus*, meaning "sexual love" and "sexual desire." Another version of the Mother Goose nursery rhyme beginning "One for sorrow" claims "Eight for a whore," a verse that doesn't appear in children's books.

Virgo, as star goddess, is identified with Ishtar the whore of Babylon, one of Venus's many names. In this avatar, she slept with the kings of earth. Recalling Venus's (Wynn's) association with the number eight, Sigrfrida warns her lover against venial lust: "I counsel thee eighthly: Beware of evil and avoid staves of falsehood. Betray no maid nor man's wife, nor lead them to shame."[2]

In the late summer sky, Virgo once sat on her throne with the harvested grain in her arms. Known as the joy of Mercury, Virgo was the last of the earth goddesses to leave her land. The world having grown too harsh for her gentle nature, she joined her sisters in the sky. The Virgin Mary, acquiring many of the attributes of her older sisters, also ascended to heaven in August. Her assumption occurred after her work on earth was finished. Her version appears in a well-known folk song, "Two, four, six, eight, Mary stands outside the gate."

Virgo is called "Astrais [. . .] and identified with Dike or Justice." As Justice, Virgo is sometimes depicted with balance scales in her hand. Regardless of her name, during the eighth month of Earth's solar calendar, the gold of her harvest—grain from her fields, and honey from her hives—was carried through the gate of her opening storehouse. Justice, a necessary component of a bountiful harvest, was dispensed at these summer gatherings. Held for two weeks in late July and early August, the purpose of the Icelandic Althing included the recital of law and the judging of disputes. In keeping the peace of Venus "there was a ban on the carrying of arms."[3]

Summertime Celebrations

The sun sign of Leo eventually replaced Virgo in the morning sky of late summer due to the precession of the equinoxes. In Ireland, Loaf Mass (August 1) was celebrated in the name of Lugh, a sun king. The Lughnasadh, held eight moons after the winter solstice, included horse races, games, and Troy-Town mazes. Lugh dedicated his August festival to his foster mother, a grain goddess who died clearing her land. Like other earth goddesses, Teiltiu left her name on the land. Her games were held around the graves of the Teltown hill.[4]

"In Pagan times tribes would hold fairs where they sold their wares, raced horses, met in athletic competition and participated in tribal conferences [. . .] Teltown marriages of a year and a day were consecrated."[5] I found no information on whether the Icelandic Althing held country weddings during their late summer gatherings. But in keeping with Venus's association with our peaceful eighth symbol, there was a ban on arms during both gatherings. "An eighth I know (most profitable to men): Whereso feud arises [. . .] I can heal it forthwith."[6]

Money in the Eighth House

The eighth house of astrology is concerned with other people's money. The Celtic festival celebrated with weddings, games, and bread baked from earth's summertime gold eventually degenerated into a British bank holiday. Although banks are still concerned with Venusian appreciation, the gates of the Bank of England are now closed on the last Monday of August.

Virgo's scales of justice (mentioned earlier) might also measure wealth. Earth's labyrinthine womb is the source of all material wealth, both grain and gold, which were once measured in Troy ounces,* and many of the wealthy Earth goddesses inspired the naming of money. In India, an *anna* is a common coin as well as a goddess (Annapurna). In Germany, there are *hellers*—Hel ruling the northern Underworld's treasures. The word *money* comes from Rome's goddess, Juno Moneta. Janus, the two-headed god of Roman gates, invented that money.[7] Unable to prevent her warring citizens from indulging in their favorite pastime, Juno agreed to fund wars, but only if they were just.

Described in our discussion of Raido, Venus' journey includes five morning risings, each in a different zodiac sign. This route, taking eight years, traces out a five- pointed star, a pentacle in the sky. Wearing this lawman's star denotes her role as keeper and transmitter of the law.

---

*The fundamental unit pre-1527 English weight system, was named after the French city Troyes. Known in the UK as "tower weights," the measurement was based on the wheat grain. The tower "wheat" grain was defined as exactly 45⁄64 (≈ 3⁄4) of the troy "barley" grain.

Venus, like Mercury, is an inferior planet traveling between the earth and the sun. She first passes in front of Earth, and then circles behind. Emerging from Earth's shadow she grows moon-like horns. Like all ancient goddesses, she has both warlike and peaceful aspects. As eighth symbol, she appears in her winsome peaceful form.

HEIMDALL'S RAINBOW BRIDGE

Heavenmount is the eighth where Heimdall
Is said to rule the sanctuaries;
The watcher of the gods with joy
Quaffs good mead in this happy house.

ELSA-BRITA TITCHENELL,
THE MASKS OF ODIN

In our alphabet, harvested souls pass through a gate on the way to the Underworld. But first they must cross the bridge. Like white shining Venus (Wynn/white), Heimdall is the whitest of the gods. As guardian of the bridge between the worlds, his home is at the end of a shimmering rainbow often identified with the Milky Way. On the Day of the Wolf, giants and monsters pass over Heimdall's shimmering bridge to destroy the northern world, but until the end, Heimdall the watcher stands guard on the rainbow stretching between Middle Earth and the land of the gods.

Fig. 18. Rainbow bridge of the Milky Way.

Bruno Gilli, ESO website.

The halls of the gods demonstrate knowledge of astronomy as well as hiding a mythic order. It is not a random action of a poet that placed Heimdall and his Milky Way at the gate of late summer.*

Most of the time it may be hidden or fully visible,
but when autumn comes, it gets immediately bright.
Even if covered over by faint clouds,
in the long run it can be clear through the long night.

Du Fu, "The Heavenly River,"
in *The Poetry of Du Fu*, vol 2

An alternate name for Heimdall is Rig, meaning "king." With the precession of the stars King Leo with his glowing red heart, Regulus, eventually administered Virgo's justice. Although he still owns the fifth house of astrology, his stars moved into our august eighth month, replacing Virgo with her sheaf of grain as ruler.

Described above, glowing Celtic Lugh celebrated his foster mother's harvest holiday in the eighth month of August. This king who gave his name to London is now "little stooping Lug," the leprechaun still guarding the gold hidden at the end of each rainbow.[8]

The Milky Way, formed from milk spilled by the cow goddess, was sprinkled with glittering straw dropped by St. Venus when she tried to retrieve her harvest stolen by St. Peter. Peter ended as another watcher by heaven's gate. Like Heimdall, he blows his horn and judges the harvest as he directs the fate of entering ghosts.

Far Travel

The German gods learned the secrets of far travel, or journeying to other realms, from Freya, Frigg's star being and yet another name for Venus. While Frigg has lost many of her Venusian qualities, "among Asiatic peoples the planet Venus excites unique reverence as the shaman's source of prophetic inspiration."[9]

*In China, after death souls also pass through the gate on the way to rebirth.

Fig. 19. Odin on throne with Ravens.
Photo by Ole Malling, Roskilde Museum.

Odin could transform his shape, lying as if dead, or asleep; but then he would change into the shape of a fish, worm, bird, or beast and set off in an instant to distant lands. Among the male gods, only Odin practiced far travel because it was an exhausting shaman's journey. Seen as unmanly, a woman's art, a man practicing it was considered sexually deviant. Above (fig. 19) shows a small statue of Odin dressed as a woman.

Eight is a number associated with the cycles of Venus, as is Odin's 8-legged horse, who could travel the Underworld. Like Odin, the tricky god Loki was a shapeshifter who could assume either sexuality. He once became a mare to seduce a giant's stallion, giving birth to Odin's horse. Without the help of his horse, the giant engaged to build the walls of Asgaard lost his bet with Odin. He had promised to quickly build the walls. In addition to his stallion, the giant mason lost both his wages and his life.

Celtic monks, who added their own variations to Germanic Mysteries, transcribed many rune manuscripts. A manuscript of German origin with a "trace of an Irish ancestor," named the eighth rune, usually written Wynn (Joy) as "Wing."[10] Possibly influenced by feathered Celtic shamans and kings travelling the River of Birds (Milky Way) on their way to the Otherworld. One wore a "speckled bird-dress with its winged flying [. . .] and he rose up in company with the fire, into the air of the heavens."[11]

Conclusion to the First Aettir

We have come to the end of the first aettir, the family belonging to the generous earth god Freyr. The earliest division of twenty-four runes into three groups of eight appears shortly after the origin of the Futhark.[12]

Even after the runes were reduced to sixteen, each family, no longer containing eight runes, still began with Freyr, Hel, and Tir. Perhaps reflecting a darker age, both Gyfu (gift) and Wunjo (joy) have disappeared from the sixteen runes of the Younger Futhark.

The gift of the seventh rune, Gyfu, contains the promise of a return to the light. Stars dying to the west at sunset are first reborn into the night sky. The next family, Hel's family, continues the path through the dark Underworld before returning to the light of the sun.

Second Aettir

Hel's Family

Eight for Heaven, Nine for hell
Mother Goose nursery rhyme

HEL'S RUNES

Number	Name	Meaning
9	Hagalaz	Hag god (Hel), hail, or heal
10	Naudiz or Nyd	Need
11	Isaz, Is, or Iss	Ice
12	Jera, Ger, or Ar	Harvest, plenty, or year
13	Ihwaz	Yew tree
14	Perth	Lot or dice box
15	Algiz	Elk (horned deity), protection, or elk sedge
16	Sowilo, Sol, Sigel	Sun or victory

After crossing heaven's rainbow bridge, the runes now bring us to Hel's domain.

The world of time and harmony began on the middle C of Tuesday, the "three's the charm," and ended on the seventh note. Having traveled past Wynn's white light of the first octave, we now continue the journey through the Underworld. In the north, the path begins with Hel as the ninth rune. The number placement of each letter hides the marks, the footprints of an ancient path out of Africa. We must follow carefully if we are to understand the secrets of runes. Modern scholars, distancing themselves from the excesses of earlier generations reincarnating as pharaohs and noble Trojans, have not bothered to learn the alchemy, the astronomy, and the number magic empowering earlier scholars discussing their Mysteries. This is a liability in uncovering their secrets.

9. Hagalaz

Hail or Heal

Variants: Hel (Hag god) Hagall, or Haegl (ᛡ, ᚺ, ᚽ)

THE HAG GODDESS

The sixteen runes of the Younger Futhark keep the mythology of the runes if not the original positions. Having deleted Gyfu and Wunjo, the Younger Futhark places Hagall (Hagalaz), the Hag and Crone* of the seventh rune, a number associated with aged Saturn. Nonetheless, Hel still rules the second group of the aettir.

Hel is the aging Hag of the north whose womb welcomes the seed of her dying children to await their return to the light. Describing a rune list whose Hag rune is glossed with letter *A*, René Derolez notes that of all the glossed runes only the Hag's rune is capitalized: "I admit there is no reason to have a capital H here."[1] A woman's womb shaped like letter A, the capital seems to imply respect due the black goddess.

---

*Hag-alaz is not usually translated Hag-god, but Alaz is a god from Turkey where Odin acquired his runes.

Hail [Hagall] is the coldest of grain;
*Christ created the world of old.**
OLD ENGLISH RUNE POEM

The letter *A* is the shape of a woman's womb as well as a cow goddess's head, giving birth to early alphabets. Within her powerful womb, treasures are kept safe for another generation. In keeping with the memories of older cow goddesses, the fey troll children of Frau Hulda (another name for the ancient goddess of the North) sport cow tails. Beautiful when they are young, Hulder folk marry among humans. The Norse, intermarrying with the beautiful Hulder maidens, need to beware of taking on trollish tendencies as they age.

The Celts placed Holly as their tree alphabet ogham in this position. Holly, sacred to Holle, Hel, Hilda, and Hulda, like the capitalized Hag's rune described above: "Of all the trees are in the wood, the Holly wears the crown."

Control of Wind and Rain

A ninth I know: If I am in need to save my ship afloat, I still the wind on the waves, and lull the whole sea.
"HAVAMAL," IN *CODEX REGIUS*

Teth (coil) is the ninth letter in the Phoenician/Hebrew alphabet. In Greece, the womb of the goddess Tethys produces rainclouds, rivers, and ocean waves. In the north, these waters belong to Hel. The well in her realm, Hvergelmir (Bubbling Spring) is the source of all rivers. Described above, Groa, called from her grave, teaches her son threatened by rising waters to turn back flood and foam to Hell.[2]

The Underworld can be hot, cold, or filled with briny water. In some traditions, the Underworld contains a labyrinth. Ninth letter Teth is translated as "coil" or "clew" as in a ball of yarn. The dictionary links *clew* with the thread helping Theseus find his way out of the Cretan labyrinth. Like

*By the time of this rune poem, Christ rather than the womb of the Creatrix has become the Creator.

other heroes, he traveled the coiling maze before returning to the light.

In Scandinavia, stone labyrinths kept the womb's coiling power over the winds and sea. Fishermen walked through them in procession before setting off "in the hope of controlling the weather, obtaining a good catch, and ensuring a safe return. They would build a stone labyrinth if the weather was too rough to venture forth in the hopes of containing the force of the storm within the coils."[3]

The womb of the earth goddess is the source of all sea storms, and knowing the proper wave runes, or *brimrúnar,* can recall the waves:

> *[Brimrúnar] learn, if well thou wouldst shelter the sail*
> *steeds out on the sea;*
> *On the stem shalt thou write, and the steering blade,*
> *And burn them into the oars;*
> *Though high be the breakers, and black the waves,*
> *Thou shalt safe the harbor seek.*
>
> "Sigrdrifumal," in *Codex Regius*

Life and Death, Darkness and Healing

The dark goddess was once a bottomless pit, a coiling cornucopia where the cold seed waited out the dying of the year. Hail grew in her womb and snow flew when Frau Hulda shook her feather bedding. Although Hel came to represent a world of terror, her name is related to "hale and hearty" and "heal." Several traditions associate the ninth symbol, as well as the second, with healing.

> *Hail is cold grain and shower of sleet and sickness of serpents.*
>
> *Hagall er kaldakorn ok krapadrífa ok snáka sótt. grando hildingr.**
>
> Glosses: *Grando* (grain), *hildingr* (warrior, child of Hild).
>
> Old Icelandic Rune Poem

*ingr-endings are quite common in Old Norse names. They indicate a patronymic form meaning "son/descendant of . . ." or just "one belonging to . . . ," "one coming from . . . ," "one of a specified kind."

Fig. 20a. Hagall.

Fig. 20b. EMT logo.
Image by Verdy.

Hild (one of the above glosses) is one of the battle Valkyries ferrying the slain to Valhalla. In the Younger Futhark, a star shape replaced the *H* shape of the older Hag rune. The star of Hagall represents a healing star, the hale and hearty symbol of EMTs shown above. Ice, brimstone (sulfur), and salt brine from the Hag's womb all contain healing qualities. One of the variant symbols for Teth is the alchemical symbol for the brine of salt.

Tombs and Travelers

According to one version of Mother Goose's counting nursery rhyme, "Nine is for hell." An alternate version declares, "Nine is for a burial." Sigrdrifa advises her lover: "I counsel thee ninthly: Care thou for corpses, wherever on earth thou findest them, be they sick-dead, or sea-dead, or weapon-dead. Make a bath for the departed man; wash his hands and head; comb him and dry him, ere he be put in coffin; and bid him sleep sweetly."[4]

Norse histories, having declared their origins in the land of Troy, often recall stories from the Trojan war. Prince Hector, a hero in Homer's Iliad, is mourned for nine days before being placed in the fires of his funeral pyre.

At the ninth hour, the dead travelers have given up the ghost. Those not returning to the circle with the eighth charm, now enter the dark through the ninth world belonging to Hel. Demoted into a demon, as guardian of tombs Hel still welcomed small children, women, sick people, and those who did not die in battle into her dark earth.

If not traveling by wagon, it took nine long nights to walk to Hel. The dead might be fitted with special hel shoes (*helskor*) for the journey. Having reached the tumulus, Hel might be petitioned to return the dead to life. The petitioner might also invoke sleeping witches and kings to rise from the dead to give advice.

DEATH IN THE SKIES

Sun kings have been incorporated into myths of the dying and rising grain. Stars of Heaven have also become hopelessly intertwined with stories of sun kings. Beginning to die in his prime after midsummer's sex magic the sun arrives at our ninth month: September's equinox. After Sun's fall, Day's light grows steadily weaker, but it will return on the winter solstice. The Sun's journey takes a year, so we will join him as High King of the twelfth rune (Ar).

Star children traveling along the ecliptic path of zodiac stars take forty days to reappear after disappearing from the sky as the heavens turn. Similarly, among the Scythians, the new dead were a "living dead" and were wheeled in a wagon around the countryside to visit their kin for forty days. After this time the dead person became a ghost and was carried into the womb of Earth. From here they might awake to grant guidance and favors.[5]

Stars following the path of Orion and Sirius are known as decan stars. Slightly south of the ecliptic traveled by the sun, stars, and planets, thirty-six decan stars rise ten days apart to count out a circle of 360 degrees. Disappearing from the western sky at sunset, they reappear in the night sky after seventy days. Each remains "in the underworld for seventy days where it purifies itself and rises on the horizon like Sirius. One is reminded [. . .] of the embalmment of Tutankhamen in which his body was prepared for burial [. . .] for seventy days, during which time hymns were chanted and prayers and spells recited for the soul of the dead."[6]

Hag's Starry Dance of Death and Rebirth

Twice a year—spring and fall—the zodiac's ecliptic intersects with the Milky Way. The legs of the Milky Way flow around the Galactic Center, the black source of the stars forming our galaxy. This starry womb lies between Scorpio and Sagittarius.* Among the twenty-seven mansions visited monthly by India's moon, this area of the sky contains Mula, the "root star" and a hag form of Kali, Time herself. Like all proper goddesses, India's black goddess dancing with her necklace of alphabet letters, takes the seed of the dying into her womb until a new world is born:† "At the end of each cycle during which one creation lasts, [Kali] gathers the seeds of the universe that is extinct, out of which a fresh creation is started."[7] Kali's festivals are celebrated in late October/November during which Scorpio rules the sky.

Freya's Necklace

Like other great goddesses, Freya owned a bright necklace named the Brisingamen. "Brisingamen is the Magick Circle and the Wheel of the year [giving] power over the cycles of the seasons."[8] The necklace was created by four dwarves named North, South, East, and West, and Freya offered them gold to purchase it. They refused the gold, and instead asked her to sleep one night with each of them. As another lusty earth goddess, she did.

FREYA AND THE DEAD

Hiding behind the pi-bald rotting Hel's fierce form, traces of an earlier, more powerful ruler of the burial mounds appear among the Norse stories. Under her many names, Freya, too, welcomed the dead. Although Freya and her older aspect as Frigg have been disassociated from Hel, they may once have been the triple goddess: mother, maiden, crone.

Far-traveling Freya flew in a feathered coat, rode a boar, or traveled in a cart drawn by cats, who have nine lives. As a magic-working

---

*The zodiac sign Sagittarius is the ninth house of Western astrology. It signifies, among other things, long journeys.

†Remembering Thor's Hall (first rune) with its 432,000 doors leading to destruction, the Black Age of the Kali Yuga lasts 432,000. This is the last age of the current world of Time.

Vanir, she practiced the art of far seeing and magic (*seidr*). Female seers, known as *volvas*,* wore cloaks of cat fur or feathers.

As described earlier in the eighth rune (Wunjo) chapter, Hel's rune appears on the womb of a goddess from Anatolian Asia. Freya, originally from the land of the fate-dispensing goddess Asia, is the owner of the Ninth Hall. "Folkvang [meadow of the host] is the ninth, and there Freya fixes allocation of seats in the hall; half the slain she chooses every day, and half Odin owns."[9]

Freya's home in her hall of Folkvang is called Sessrumnir (Rich in Seats), which is the name of a boat. The rich were buried in actual boats: instead of walking, they might comfortably sail to the Otherworld along the river of heaven. The spinning Nyd sticks, following as the tenth rune, were used to set the boat on fire. The higher the flames, the faster the soul could rise to the afterlife. For those not rich enough to be buried in a boat, stones were placed around the burial mounds in the shape of boats to help sail the sky.

Fig. 21. Stone Boat. Anundshög, Västerås.

Christer Johansson.

*This word was taken from the medieval Latin word *volva* or *vulva*, meaning "womb," or "female genitals."

Freya the Healer

As seen at the beginning of this chapter, the "sickness of serpents" and healing are intertwined within the ninth rune. When discussing the second Ur rune, I described the nine healing twigs (wuldortanas), which Odin took to defeat the serpent of illness.

Healing magic underlies the Earth magic eventually adapted to the needs of warriors. Freya/Frigg was goddess of married women and marriage, and childbearing was always a gamble. Her name (often replaced by Mary) names numerous healing plants: "[Freya] helped women give birth to children, and as Scandinavians used the plant lady's bedstraw (*Galium verum*) as a sedative, they called it Frigg's grass."[10] Placed in the beds of women giving birth, it was also called Freyja's grass. But we have just entered nine's swirling womb of the Underworld. We must wait until the 16th rune to welcome back Earth's Sun.

10. Naudiz

Need

Variants: Nyd, Nauðr, or Nauthiz

Nyd constricts the heart, but it often serves as a help and salvation to the sons of man if they heed it in time.

Old English Rune Poem

Nauðr (Need) gives scant choice; a naked man is chilled by the frost.

Old Norwegian Rune Poem

JUDGMENTS ARRIVE WITH THE DECIMATIONS OF TIME

Glistener is the tenth, its pillars are of gold, and it is thatched with silver: here Forseti (Judge) lives every day, settling all causes.

"Grimnismal," Vigfusson and Powell trans.

Naudiz, the tenth rune (eighth in the Younger Futhark), is a spinning letter of fate, fire, and judgment. Her stories correspond to summer's end. Halloween is celebrated in our tenth month, and Yom Kippur, the

Jewish Day of Atonement, occurs ten days after the Jewish New Year in the fall. Ten's magic contains the compulsion of time, retribution for past deeds, and dissolution of the manifest body before a coming rebirth. We now stand in the hand of God, hand (Yod) being the tenth Hebrew letter, waiting for our soul to be judged.

Forseti, the judge of the gods, rules the Tenth Hall: "Whoever come to him [Forseti] with difficult legal disputes, they all leave with their differences settled. It is the best place of judgment among gods and men."[1] Although Forseti is usually translated as "the presiding one" or "judge," in *Teutonic Mythology*, Jacob Grimm derived Forseti from *fors*, a "whirling stream."[2] Thus, included among Naudiz's attributes are judgments and the spinning magic of the Mill of Fate slowly grinding out justice and retribution.

Spinning Magic

The turning Mill of Fate grinds slowly but exceedingly fine as the gold of summer blood-reddens with the coming winter. One must share Earth's blessings to avoid a fatal retribution. What goes around Time's wheel, comes around.

Hulda, also known as Frau Holle or Holda, the ancient Germanic goddess we met in our discussion of Hagalaz, is associated with spinning and agriculture, and her festivals were held in the winter. Her women would leave their houses, riding their distaffs out into the silence of the night. They would travel vast distances through the sky to great feasts or to thundering battles amongst the clouds.*

Seidr or seiðr, the practice of Norse visionary magic, is also thought to involve spinning. This might explain why imagery of the distaff—a tool used in spinning flax or sometimes wool—have been found on staffs buries with a number of Norse women.[3] In the Saga of Erik the Red, a *seiðkona* or *vǫlva* in Greenland named Thorbjǫrg carried one such a distaff (*seiðstafr*), "ornamented with brass, and inlaid with gems round about the knob."[4]

*Known as Diana Rides, they are described in the *Canon Episcopi*, (c. 1000).

While most people travel to the Otherworld only after death, witches, magicians, and eventually Odin learned to use seidr to travel beyond their mortal coil. To avoid losing their way home, dreaming witches created a silver thread spun out from their navel. If this thread was broken, she was lost, and her soul wandered aimlessly, unable to return home: "The tenth I know: If I see witches [hedge-riders] dancing in the air, I prevail so that they go astray and cannot find their own skins and their own haunts."[5]

Losing one's way in this fashion may explain the practice of whirling a finger pointed at one's head to indicate that one has gone berserk, gone out of body, out of mind.

Arrival of the Fates

Originally, northern gods had no fatal judgments, only gold and pleasure until three giant women arrived. Then, they made laws there, and "life was allotted to the sons of men and set their fates."[6] Although northern warriors might still sail off to enjoy battle, and their dead heroes might still be rewarded by a heaven filled with games, drink, and war, they must now face judgment for their actions.

As described in the Uruz chapter, the World Tree supporting the nine realms of the northern world has three roots. The root of the world of the gods (Asgaard) contains the well of Urd, home of the three fate-bestowing women. Scandinavians knew the three as Norns: "Weird [Urd] they called the first of them. The second, Becoming [Verdandi] they carved on a tablet . . . [and] Should [Skuld/Debt] the third."[7] In many depictions of the triple women, the middle goddess is shown holding her book. Her moving finger, recording the fee, writes life's measurements. The payment will be collected by the eleventh hour, debts coming due before midnight.

The association of three with deities assigning fate is very ancient. The classic Roman Fates were known as Nona (nine), Decima (ten), and Morta (eleven). These three measured out the thread of life from birth to death. In ancient Sumer, thousands of years before the Roman Fates, three stars (the MUL sign) were written before all words signifying a celestial object. Each star in that tradition represented a god, and the three have an "innate association with fate assigning destiny."[8]

Fire Magic

Nyd is another name for Naudiz. Nyd sticks are wooden sticks twirled together to start ritual fires. In a rare description of a Viking burial by Ahmad ibn Fadlan, an Arab historian in the tenth century, the dead man was buried for nine days (Remember the "Nine's for a burial" in the previous chapter). On the tenth he was dug up and, after sacrifice and ritual, was burned in his boat. Unfortunately, the Arab historian did not describe the method used to start the fire.

Only a few could far travel before Death released the soul from the mortal body. Most waited for the loosening of death to open the way. Later people, too impatient to wait for the slow alchemy of a body dissolving into black earth, discovered the magic of fire in speeding the dissolution. Smoke had the power to carry souls, prayers, and astral travelers up the chimney into the waiting heavens, and the friction of spinning Nyd sticks could generate the fire.

In India the Hindu god of death and justice, Yama, was the first man to die, marking out the path for others to follow. His sister, the River Yamuna, preceded him into the Otherworld. Like the Norse Forseti living in the Tenth Hall of Norse gods, Yama judged souls entering the realm of death. At first, humans had to walk the long miles to the land of the dead; then Yama, like other Indo-European gods, learned to release the soul more quickly through the use of fire. Yama's priest is Agni, literally "fire" himself. He was born "of friction between . . . a male and a female fire-stick."[9]

THE GODDESS OF TIME

The calendar has brought us to the dying of the year. The tombs of the dead stand open, and the veil between the worlds grows thin. Having been culled and judged, the dead discard their physical form and travel further into the Underworld. Those who have not yet found passage into a new life emerge briefly to visit their kin.

Winter's goddess now dances, shaking apart a dying world. The center no longer holds. Decima, the Crone aspect of Time, is the strongest of the goddesses, for all are consumed in her fires. This season belongs to Kali, black goddess of time, whose decimations are celebrated in late October and to the wolfish Nemesis, as Divine Retribution: "Nemesis [chases the sacred king as] he goes through his seasonal transformations [. . .] indicated on the spokes of Nemesis' wheel."[10]

Nemesis means "to give what is due." Due as Debt is the third Norn. It is the fire-eyed Goddess of Retribution whose eye burns at the center of the stars revolving over the World Tree. Aging Fortune, not light-hearted Lady Luck, spins this Wheel. In the agricultural calendar, seed grain is judged, measured, parched, and ground along with dying souls by the whirling fire-magic of this letter.

PAYING ONE'S DEBT: THE WHEEL OF FATE

> *Naud the grief of the bondmaid and state of oppression and toilsome work.*
>
> *Nauð er Þýjar þrá ok þungr kostr ok vássamlig verk. opera niflungr.*
> Glosses: *Opera* (work), *Niflungr* (descendant of the Nibelungs)
>
> Old Icelandic Rune Poem

The spinning and gold associations of Naud appears in the myth of King Frodi (a.k.a. Freyr). He once acquired two giant women—Menia and Fenia—as bondmaids and had them turning a great millstone. At first, they ground gold, peace, and good harvests. Greedy for more gold, he refused to let them rest despite their pleading fatigue. But as daughters of ancient mountain giants, they then ground out an army, which slaughtered the king. However, they were carried off by the victor and forced to continue grinding. But this time they ground out salt, sinking their boat and creating a spinning whirlpool.*

The story of the Niflungr (Nibelungs), descendants of the mist people, contains the same greed for gold that destroyed Frodi. The gold had been acquired to pay a wergild for killing a man. The river gold and its ring, cursed when it was stolen from a dwarf, brought death to all who possessed it. The gold caused brother to kill brother, mother to kill her sons, and lovers to be betrayed. The greed for the cursed gold ultimately killed the Nibelung Gunnar, Sigurd's brother-in-law, who broke his oath sworn to Sigurd. His lover, Sigrdrifa, warns him: "I counsel thee tenthly: Trust thou never the oath of an outlaw's son, if thou hast slain his brother, or felled his father. There is a wolf in a young son, though he be comforted with gold."[11] Sigurd, having stolen the gold from a dragon, was also among its victims.

After Sigrdrifa's (Brynhild's) death, "two pyres were made, one was for Sigurd and that was kindled first, and Brynhild was burnt on the second one, and she was in a wagon."[12] After death, Brynhild set out by wagon to join her lover in Hel.

So it seems that Naudiz's judgments can be harsh for hording gold. Better to share one's fortune with a tithe: the one out of ten parts given in charity.

---

*The swirling pool is called the Saltstraumen. It is the world's largest maelstrom and located off the west coast of Norway.

11. Isaz

Ice

Variants: Is, Iss, or Ísa

Ice is very cold and exceedingly slippery; it glistens, clear as glass, very much like gems.

Old English Rune Poem

AN ICY PAUSE

I have become like a bottle in the smoke [. . .] how much longer must I wait?

11th Hebrew letter, Kaph,
Psalm 119, verse 81–88

Having risen on the flames of the burning pyre, we must now pause to get our bearings and to let the smoke clear. We have arrived at the eleventh rune (ninth in the Younger Futhark) of icy stasis: The third goddess of fate: Morta (eleven), following her sisters Nona (nine) and Decima (ten), demands a pause before continuing the journey.

Ice and Crystal Reflections

K is the angle of reflection equal to the angle of incidence.

VICTOR HUGO, "TRAVEL NOTEBOOKS," IN *WRITING: THE STORY OF ALPHABETS AND SCRIPTS,* BY GEORGES JEAN, 1992

We are exactly halfway through the twenty-two letters of the Hebrew/Phoenician alphabet. The eleventh Phoenician letter Kaph (palm of hand) was originally written ꓘ as the reverse or reflection of the eleventh English letter *K* ꓘ.

Among the 22 letters of the Hebrew/Phoenician alphabet, we are exactly halfway. 11 being the twin to 1, represents both 1 + 1 as 2, and 1 + 1 as 11. Isaz, the ice rune, is written like numeral 1 and as a proper twin, it is reflective: 1 - 1, or 11. The choice of the eleventh rune is the reflective mirror of ice.

Adam, the first man, is made of red earth, and the pressure of his passage through the blue Underworld creates adamantine diamonds from his embers. These diamonds keep company with nearby crystals. According to Pliny the Elder (23–79 CE), shimmering quartz crystals, like "unripe diamonds,"[1] were formed from ice (11th rune). Like ice and the letter *K*, crystals are reflective, and when held up to light or rubbed together, they produce rainbows leading to the Otherworld. Quartz crystal "radios" were believed to be useful in communicating between the worlds: "The use of quartz as a device to communicate with nonhuman or nonliving things extends around the globe and seems to form part of an essentially animistic attitude to the experienced world."[2]

Boars and Protection

Ice: bark of rivers and roof of the wave and destruction of the doomed.

Íss er árbörkr ok unnar þak ok feigra manna fár. glacies jöfurr.
Glosses: *Glacies* (ice), *jöfurr* (prince; originally meant wild boar)

OLD ICELANDIC RUNE POEM

Preceding the Day of the Wolf—when gods to destruction go—is the Fimbulwinter, the mighty winter. Giants and demons come from the land of ice, others from the land of fire, riding over the rainbow bridge toward the doom of Ragnarok. Until these battles, warriors were protected by the eleventh charm: "I know an eleventh if I have to lead long loyal friends into battle; under the shields I chant, and they journey confidently, safely to the battle, safely from the battle, safely they comeback from everywhere."[3] They were also protected by their boar helms.

Boars are mentioned in the gloss of the OIRP. The boar helm, one of Freyr's treasures, was worn by German tribes as a defense: "They worship the Mother of the gods, and wear, as an emblem of this cult, the device of a wild boar, which stands them instead of armour or human protection and gives the worshipper a sense of security even among his enemies."[4]

The Swedish warrior Beowulf implies that "when the hefted sword, its hammered edge slathered in blood, razes the sturdy boar-ridge off a helmet,"[5] it promises the death of the wearer. Greeks also valued fierce boar helms to protect the warrior from death: "Over his head he set a helmet made of leather. Inside it was crisscrossed taut with many

Fig. 22. Mycenaean boar tusk helmet, fourteenth century BCE.

National Museum, Athens. Photo courtesy of Jebulon.

thongs, outside the gleaming teeth of a white-tusked boar [. . .] a master craftsman's work."[6]

The Eleventh Hour

> *I counsel thee eleventhly [. . .] For thee I can forecast no long life. Mighty feuds have arisen which will cause thy death.*
>
> "Sigrdrifumal," in *Corpus Poeticum Boreale*, Vigfusson and Powell trans.

The shadow of the bright sun, having passed through 1-1's gate, now travels deeper into the dark. In Egypt, the upraised palms of Kaph (palm) depict the being known as Ka ⊔ who represents the Underworld traveler's shadow twin. Time's darkening spirit is a magician slipping through the gap between one breath and the next.

The eleventh hour brings us closer to the hour of the wolf, the destruction of the doomed, the dying of the year. Both Nemesis and wolfish Var demand debts to be paid before moving on. Debt (Skuld) is the third Germanic Norn, and Death (Morta) is the third Greek Fate—the ultimate fee paid by the living.

The old German calendar recognized the eleventh month of November as slaughter month. Similarly, we remember the dead of the First World War on November 11 (11/11), Armistice Day, with blood-red poppies. Opium made from poppies, associated with both dreaming and death, offers another way to travel the Otherworld.

St. Martin, whose Danish name is Mortin, was buried on November 11 in France. Martinmas, the feast day of St. Martin held on the eleventh of November, was the day of the final culling and slaughtering of mortal animals: "a custom prevailed [. . .] of killing cows, oxen, swine, etc., at this season, which were cured for the winter."[7] This is the time Earth briefly pauses before winter whitens her land. St. Martin spreads a red coat of leaves over a beggared Earth, and with its warmth, there is a brief stay of good weather before the snow arrives.

Fig. 23. Drawing of the motif of a gold ring from Mycenae c. 1450 BCE, depicting a goddess holding three opium poppies.
Unknown author.

Resting Ships and Sailing Saints

Sagittarius rising in our eleventh month of November provides yet another passage to the Underworld after death. Those who don't want to ride may travel by foot or wing, by smoke, or wagon. They may travel by ship that sails the River of Stars.

Mora, according to Isidore of Seville, meant "time out." And the fish, remora, also provides a kind of time out: "Remora [. . .] gets its name because it holds a ship fast [. . .] The Latins call this fish by the name of Mora because it compels vessels to stay motionless."[8]

> *The eleventh hall is Njorth's which he built and named Noatun [Ship's Rest].*
>
> "Grimnismal," Crawford trans.

Many of the saints of early winter relate to sailing. St. Catherine is associated with the ship's star Canopus. St. Clement, patron of both

Fig. 24. The anchor is created by Vulcans in the shape of Sagittarius's arrow.
Rogers Anchor, 1911. Courtesy of Encyclopedia Britannica, 11th ed.

Vulcans and anchor makers, was killed when he was thrown into the sea with an anchor tied around his neck. Anchors, of course, hold a boat at ship's rest in the water. Like these saints, Njorth (Njord), ruler of the sea, protects sailors.

Apple Celebrations of Fall

Both St. Clement (November 23) and St. Catherine (November 25) are celebrated with fall's apples. Their festivals include drinking and sharing apples ripening at this time of year. An English folk rhyme relates: "Catt'n and Clement comes year by year, some of your apples and some of your beer."[9]

The fateful Morta (11) as icy Death gets her name "from 'morsu,' that bite of the first man when munching fruit from the forbidden tree [. . .]"[10] After being expelled from Eden in the fall of man he entered the world of death. Adam stood weeping in the river for forty days before winter's sun was reborn (winter solstice), giving him the courage to emerge. Adam's apple is forever lodged in his throat.

The association of apples with the pause mandated by number eleven may contain memories of calendar rectification. The lunar calendar of 354 days is 11 days shorter than the solar calendar of 365. According to E. C. Krupp in *Beyond the Blue Horizon*, the race of the huntress Atalanta reflected this rectification when she lost a race by stopping to pick up three apples dropped by her opponent. Every 8 years, 3 additional months (Atalanta's three apples) must be added to equate the lunar and solar calendars (8 + 3 = 11). Krupp says that this "reconciliation of the sun and moon is more than just an affair of the heart. It's a ritual requirement for seasonal ceremonies and festivals."[11]

Fig. 25. Watermark of a boar with an apple in its mouth, bearing a *K* upon his back.

From Bayley, *Lost Language of Symbolism*, 89.

Nemesis, whose name translates as "what is due," lives behind the right ear whispering morality along with mortality and carries an apple bough. Her younger avatar, Artemis/Diana, has a home among the arrow stars of Sagittarius. As Diana Nemetona, she was also represented with an apple bough.

CROSS OF THE ECLIPTIC

Sagittarius rises in our eleventh month of November, when the cross of the ecliptic intersects the Milky Way first near the twins of Gemini and Orion and then near Sagittarius and Scorpio. The River of Stars flowing between these constellations splits into a broad and narrow path near the Galactic Womb, necessitating a choice: "The road [. . .] divides and they must choose which to take. Forked ways in the Land of the Death are to be found in the Mystery Religions and were known to the Pythagoreans."[12] It is the broad road that leads to Hell (Galactic Womb).

> *Is (Ice) we call the broad bridge; the blind man must be led.*
>
> Old Norwegian Rune Poem

We are now moving toward Twelfth Night. The boar's head with an apple in its mouth will be carried into the feast hall with ceremony. The boar sacrifice, the *sonarblot*, dedicated to the generous Freyr, occurs on the winter solstice, our twelfth month.

12. JERA

HARVEST OR PLENTY

Variants: Ár (Year) or Ger (ᛄ, ᛃ)

Ger is a joy to men, when God, the holy King of Heaven, suffers the earth to bring forth shining fruits for rich and poor alike.

OLD ENGLISH RUNE POEM

THE TWELFTH NIGHT

One of the names for the twelfth rune (tenth in the Younger Futhark) is Ar, meaning "year." Ar is "early used for the dead patriarchs who are supposed to give good seasons."[1]

Plenty (Ár) boon to men and good summer and thriving crops.

Ár er gumna góði ok gott sumar algróinn akr. annus allvaldr.
Glosses: *Annus* (year), *allvaldr* (king or ruler)

OLD ICELANDIC RUNE POEM

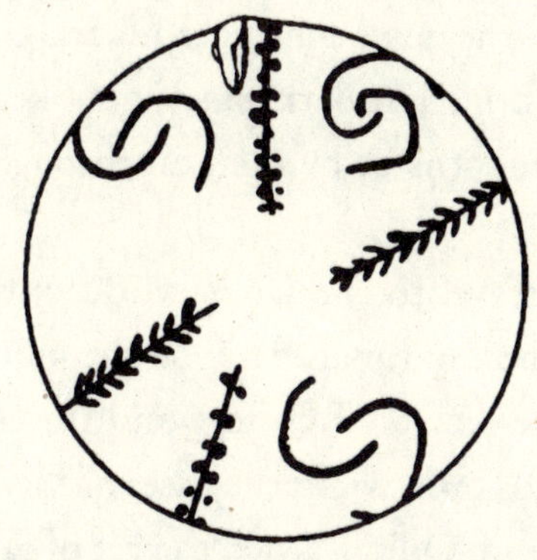

Fig. 26. Pendant, Albania, c. 4500 BCE.
Gimbutas, *The Language of the Goddess*, 295.

Because the king was ultimately responsible for the wealth of his land, his trip to the Otherworld sometimes included a physical sacrifice. The "little death" of sexuality enacted when he married his land became a physical death as his power faded: "All agreed that the times of scarcity were on account of their king, and they resolved to offer him for good seasons, and to assault and kill him, and sprinkle the stalls of the gods with his blood."[2]

By the twelfth charm, El (*L* as in the twelfth letter in the English alphabet), potent owner of the third charm, has been harvested and hung upside down. The Old Hebrew/Phoenician alphabet's third letter ᒣ (Gimel) becomes the alphabet's twelfth letter ∠ (Lamed) ruler, creating the symbol for Jera ᛃ.

The symbol depicted on the pendant shown above appeared thousands of years before the arrival of runes. Reversed at the twelfth hour, his world turned upside down, the Sun now begins traveling backward through time and space. After a brief standstill on the twelfth month's winter solstice, the sun literally reverses and begins moving north toward summer.

Communing with the Otherworld

> *I know a twelfth spell: if I see hanging from a tree, a dead man's corpse, I carve some runes and paint them, and then that corpse will walk and speak with me.*
>
> "Havamal," Crawford trans.

Having discarded his mortal coil, the journeyman continues his travels through the eight runes of Hel's Underworld. The dark journey is taken yearly by John Barleycorn* over twelve months or by the Sun through the night's twelve hours.

As mentioned earlier, most people travel to the Underworld only after the thread of life is cut, but witches and magicians might journey there at will. Eventually learning the secrets of Otherworld travel, kings as well as poets sat on burial mounds or between the gates of their high-seat pillars to commune with the dead. Odin learned the art of far seeing from the Vanir.

Whether dead or alive and dreaming by the tombs of their ancestors, kings made the journey both for inspiration and to feed their winter-hungry people. The ruler as sun, barley, or vine king dies symbolically, or literally, turned upside down on the stroke of midnight. But the dying ember of time as twelfth letter *L*'s ruling King El will eventually rejoin the dance.

ASTROLOGY, ALCOHOL, AND RISING SPIRITS

The weapon-blessed Odin lives on wine alone.

"Grimnismal," Vigfusson and Powell trans.

The twelfth (and last) house of astrology belongs to Pisces, home of martyrs, drinkers, healers, and psychic travelers. Another aspect of Pisces is that "it is both an end and a beginning. The zodiac is [a helix]; each time one goes around, one has also moved up."[3]

Neptune now rules Pisces.† While this bull and Earth Shaker was once husband of Earth, he won a new domain by lottery, and like the Norse Njord, became a sea god. In the northern tradition, the god of the sea owns the cauldron in which the "merry brew" was prepared.

*John Barleycorn is the personification of the barley crop harvested in late fall and the beer later made from it.

†Some claim Jupiter, which takes twelve years to circle the zodiac, is still the true ruler of Pisces.

Norse Aegir and his wife Ran lived at the bottom of the sea. Known for their hospitality, they served drinks to drowned sailors and visiting gods, brewing beer for the thirsty in their mile-wide cauldron obtained from a giant.

Beer wasn't the only spirit brewed in the ancient world. Greeks, integrating new and old festivals, celebrated the month of Poseidon (Neptune) in December with a wine festival in honor of the vine king or god of wine, Dionysus. Wine grapes originated in Turkey, the lands of Asia where Odin discovered his runes. The oldest known winery was found in Armenia where Noah, shortly after landing his ark, drank himself into oblivion.*

A grandson of Cadmus, Dionysus traveled between India and Britain to transmit the Mysteries of "spirits." Eventually, he "possessed himself of the festivals of Demeter, took over her threshing floor, and compelled the anomaly of a winter threshing festival."[4] This was a celebration that took place around the time when the harvested grain was threshed, and the edible part of the grain was separated from the chaff—the time when John Barleycorn (barley) sacrificed his seed to assist the raising of spirits:† "There was three men come out o' the west their fortunes for to try. And these three men made a solemn vow: John Barleycorn must die."

SACRIFICE FOR THE LAND'S PROSPERITY

As the sacrificial boar, with mouth stuffed with an apple, the king is consumed along with other spirits over the twelve days of Christmas.

> *Plenty (Ar) is a boon to men; I say Frothi [Frodi] was generous.*
>
> Old Norwegian Rune Poem

*Wine literally preserves from death: The effect of wine is "truly bactericidal, not bacteriostatic." (Manjo, 1975, 186–88) That is, it kills off bacteria. The property is specific to wine and wine vinegar, rather than to alcohol.

†When barley is fermented, it becomes beer.

High King Yngvi (a.k.a. Freyr or Frodi) was the ancestor of numerous peoples including the Ynglings. His descendants, like those of many kings, were sacrificed for good seasons: his son drowned in a cauldron of ale, and his grandson died after marrying the daughter of Snow. Other Yngvis were sacrificed after bad harvests, hung until dead by the daughter of Frost, killed by a nightmare, or by peasants wielding hayforks. "The Great Dag [Day] fell by the hayfork of a base thrall," and his son rode a wooden horse to Hel, hanging on a gallows horse like other sacrificed High Kings.[5] But as High King, Freyr returns as each new king of the land.

Presiding over fertility, sunlight, and rain, Freyr was the husband of the frost giantess Gerd (garden), who we first met in our discussion of the sixth rune Kenaz. Gerd was a Bride of the Land that northern kings married to gain legitimacy. Seeding her moist dark furrows resulted in the gold of summer harvest to feed the king's people. To improve this harvest, a boar was sacrificed on the winter solstice in the hope of garnering Freyr's generous favors.

13. Ihwaz

Yew Tree

Variants: *Eihwaz, Eibwaz, or Iwaz*

THE PROMISE OF DEATH AND REBIRTH

Ihwaz, the thirteenth rune, contains a promise both of death and of rebirth. Often planted by graveyards, the yew tree, keeper of the flame, was once the coffin of the vine. Yew barrels stored the spirits of wine until their release in the spring. The wood of yew (Taxus), being intensely toxic, was a poor choice since some wine drinkers died. In Greece, Hermes released the wine-blue spirits* in February: Opening the wine jars allowed spirits to reenter the world.

The Younger Futhark changed the number and sometimes the order of the Elder Futhark runes. The Old Norwegian Rune Poem placed Ihwaz as the last (sixteenth) rune. I am keeping the order of the Elder Futhark runes here. The yew tree as the thirteenth symbol is a number both of finality and rebirth of the sun king out of the rising waters of thirteen's watery Deluge.

*"Spirits" have long been used to describe both alcohol and souls. All alcohol burns blue. The purer the source, the bluer the flame. Hermes, as the messenger god, is uniquely positioned to navigate these otherworldly intersections.

Fig. 27. Hermes releasing the spirits.

Jane Harrison, *Prologomena*, 1903 (Princeton, 1991), 43.

Death may come by fire and water or come riding in the moonlight on a pale horse. Freya sometimes wore a horse mask. Her Celtic sister is the great mare Epona whose festival was celebrated in January. Epona waited near water or by cemeteries or went riding past the tumuli of the sleeping dead. Carrying returning souls back to the tumescent wombs of hopeful mothers, the sounds of her galloping horse can be heard (and felt) after the fifth month of pregnancy.

The winter Disablot, a celebration honoring female spirits and deities, was held on the first full moon after the winter solstice: "The yearly Disablot in winter [the season for ancestor worship] for good seasons [the special gift of the dead], and from the obvious necessity of the dead of womankind being provided for, we believe that 'Dis' was a proper name for a female spirit."[1]

The foolishness of the twelve days of Christmas past, the dying ember of time winks out on the darkest day of a dying year. The Wheel has carried us to Mother's Night to await the rebirth of her winter son. Out of the waters of Earth's womb will sail yet again an arc carrying the returning son. The Star Child is reborn time without end, emerging from his mother's womb to shine over the World Tree.*

*In various mythologies and traditions, star children are those that arrive in this world with preternatural knowledge.

Protective Waters

> *I know a thirteenth if I must pour water over a young warrior; he will not fall though he goes into battle, before swords that man will not sink.*
>
> "Havamal," Carolyne Larrington trans.

The "water" referred to in the thirteenth charm above may have been vinegar, which is brewed by adding a "mother" (a form of yeast and bacteria) to wine. When applied to wool, this vinegar helped to create a protective garment. According to Pliny, "Wool is compressed also for making a felt, which, if soaked in vinegar, is capable of resisting even iron; and, what is still more, after having gone through the last process, wool will even resist fire."[2]

SEASONS AND CYCLES

The moon orbits the earth thirteen times during a solar year with the spirit-blue moon being the thirteenth. The star of Freya (Venus) also has a cycle involving thirteen. Venus circles between the earth and sun, spending 236 days as a morning star, which is often seen as either male or Venus in her fierce aspect. After hiding for 90 days, she reappears as the gentle evening star for 250 days, the 9 months of human pregnancy, before disappearing for 8 days.

Described in Chapter 5, Venus has five heliacal risings, each in a different zodiac sign, creating a pentacle over eight years. During those eight years, winsome Freya/Venus orbits the earth thirteen times. As horned moon, another of her aspects, she circles 13 times per 12-month solar year, the thirteenth being the blue moon.

After the northern gods die on the Day of the Wolf, only the goddess Freya survived. The ancient Mother may have lost her power, but even in the Black Age, the Goddess' death was inconceivable: "Freya alone remained of the gods and she became on this account celebrated that all women of distinction were called by her name whence they have the title Frue."[3]

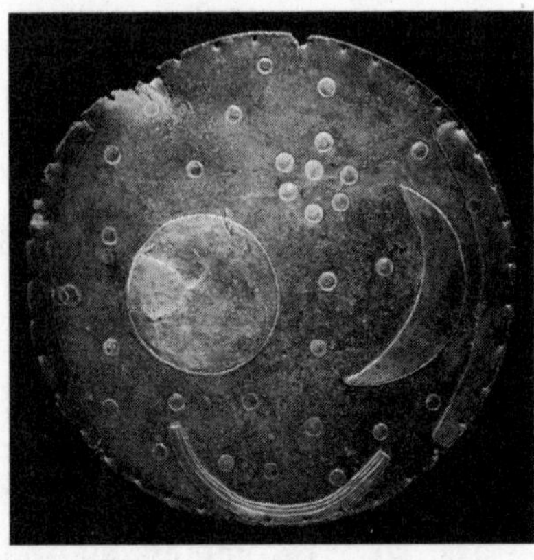

Fig. 28. Nebra sky disc, Germany, c. 1600 BCE.

Photo courtesy of Dbachmann.

The number thirteen is important in calendars rectification—the addition of a thirteenth month to the lunar year. According to the Babylonian calendar (c. 500 BCE), a thirteenth month should be added to the lunar year at certain times to keep the lunar calendar in sync with the seasons. The disc of Nebra (shown above) was apparently used as an astronomical clock to determine the exact times for doing this: "A thirteenth month should be added to the lunar calendar only when one sees the constellation of the moon and the Pleiades exactly as they appear on the Nebra sky disc."[4]

The disc was found near Europe's oldest known observatory in Goseck, Germany. Attesting to the wide-ranging trade of the ancient world, the gold and tin used in its construction came from Cornwall, England.[5]

THE WORLD TREE

> *Yew is a tree with rough bark, hard and fast in the earth, supported by its roots, a guardian of flame, and a joy upon an estate.*
>
> OLD ENGLISH RUNE POEM

As with all myths, there are multiple origins. The placental tree of life grows between the navel of each returning child and the watery well of his mother's womb. Another World Tree belongs to each newly delivered child. The spinal column has 24 vertebrae, the number of the hours of the turning dark and bright fortnights of each year, and of the Elder Futhark runes. Inside this tree is the spinal cord. Two nerves branch from each vertebra. At the head is an opening in the skull for illumination to enter and the enlightened soul to exit. At the base, the nerves form a tangle of roots travelling down to well-planted feet.

YEW AS THE FINAL RUNE OF THE YOUNGER FUTHARK (16 RUNES)

While I have been concentrating on the 24 runes of the Elder Futhark, I need to explore the deadly Yew as the final symbol in the Younger Futharks. In this position, it refers to winter and death.

> *YR (Yew) is the greenest of trees in winter; it is wont to crackle when it burns.*
>
> NORWEGIAN RUNE POEM

> *YR (Yew) bent bow and brittle iron and giant of the arrow [Farbauti].*
>
> *Ýr er bendr bogi ok brotgjarnt járn ok fífu fárbauti. arcus ynglingr.*
> Glosses: *arcus* (bow) *ynglingr.* (Descendent of *Ing*/ young *Ing*)
>
> OLD ICELANDIC RUNE POEM

The trickster god, Loki (wildfire), was fathered by the arrow giant Farbauti (Cruel Striker, which refers to lightning) and Laufey (Full of Leaves). Lightning hitting leaves generates Loki's fire. This stone shows a possible image of Loki on a hearthstone used to protect the bellows. He had his lips sewn together after losing a bet with magician smiths.

Fig. 29. Snaptun Stone, Denmark c. 1000 CE.
Moesgard Museum, Denmark, Photo by Bloodofox.

One of Loki's children is a giant worm, an ouroboros encircling the Norse world with its tail in its mouth. When this Midgard serpent lets go of his tail, that world will end. The ocean will surge up on to the lands because the Midgard serpent will fly into a giant rage and make its way ashore, "The sun will go dark; earth sink into the sea."[6] The circling serpent holding its tail implies the continual cycle back into the world; when it lets go, the Wheel of this cycle can no longer roll.

The actions of Loki's fierce child ultimately end in the destruction of the northern world, but ancient earth magic offered a return from death. Out of this destruction, a new green world will rise; a new generation will emerge.

14. Perth

Dice Box

Variants: Peorð

I know a fourteenth if I have to reckon up the gods before a group of men: of Asir and elves I know every detail, few who are not wise know that.

"Havamal," Carolyne Larrington trans.

Peorð is a source of recreation and amusement to the great, where warriors sit blithely together in the banqueting-hall.

Old English Rune Poem

ALLOTMENT OF FORTUNE

After the thirteenth blue moon, out of the waters of ending, emerges a hero. With his return over the waters of the Deluge, knowledge and measurements must be passed on. A reckoning must be allotted to a new generation. When each new world rises from the waters of the Deluge, the inheritance of fortune and land must be redistributed.

The waters of the thirteenth Phoenician letter Mem (water) now deliver a fish as the fourteenth symbol—the Phoenician letter Nun

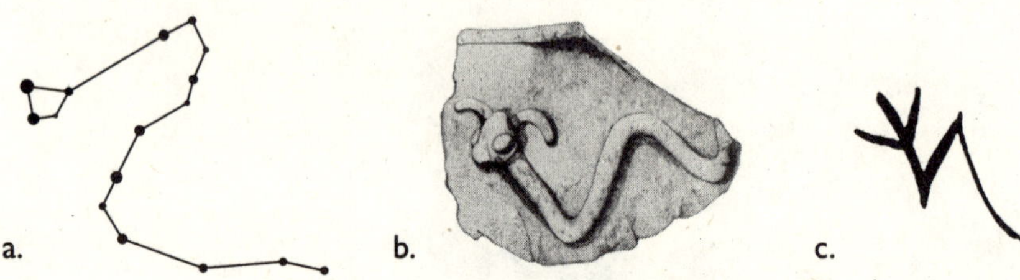

Fig. 30a. Image of the Dragon's constellation (Draco).
Fig. 30b. A 6000-year-old shard.
Fig. 30c. A copy of the South Iberian letter for nun (fish).
Fig. 30a. Dirk Hunniger.
Fig. 30b. From Gimbutas, *Civilization of the Goddess*, 237.
Fig. 30c. From Diringer, *The Alphabet*, vol. 2, 174.

(fish or serpent). Both Pisces (the fish) and the number fourteen are associated with gambling used to reckon this allotment. The fourteenth rune, Perth, is a dice box for casting lots.

Gambling and Lots in the Ancient World

Having emerged from the zodiac waters of Aquarius, the sky's pattern now returns to February. The early spring Festival of Lots (Purim), celebrating the Israelites escape from death now approaches. The festival is named for the lots that Haman cast to determine the day on which he would kill the Jews—the plan foiled by Queen Esther. It is celebrated on the fourteenth day of the Hebrew month of Adar, which usually falls in February.

Similarly, the gods of ancient Greece, having overthrown an older rule of giants, divided their world by gambling: Neptune (Poseidon) ruling Pisces won the sea and Jupiter won the sky. And when a Christian zodiac was created to replace the pagan ruler of Pisces, St. Matthias, also selected by a lottery, was given ownership.

Egypt's Thoth, a deity associated with writing and measures, created a 365-day calendar (improving the 360-day calendar) by gambling. He won five extra days by winning from the moon: 1/72nd of its light (360/72 = 5). Each extra day contained about 1/14th of her light.

Fig. 31. Pisces and a game board on the zodiac of Dendera, Egypt, c. first century BCE.
Photographer unknown.

In northern lands the gods also played games of chance:

In their dwellings at peace they played at tables,
Of gold no lack did the gods then know,
Til thither came up giant-maids three,
Huge of might, out of Jotunheim.

"Voluspo," in *The Poetic Edda*,
Bellows trans.

"The exact nature of the game, and whether it more closely resembled chess or checkers, has been made the subject of 400-page theses, Willard Fiske's *Chess in Iceland*."[1] Chessboards have 64 black and white squares and a "hex" of 6 players: King, Queen, Bishop, Knight, Rook and Pawn.

The Great Square of Pegasus—a large easily spotted pattern of stars in Pisces—was used by celestial gamblers for playing at lots.[2] "The draught board, which seems to have been introduced into Egypt from

Babylonia, was used in connection with astrology, and later the dead made use of it when playing against [. . .] the serpent god."[3] Gambling and lotteries was often a means of distributing inheritance to another generation.

THE SERPENT GOD

A horned dragon—Draco—once circled the North Star. Deposed by the precession (the slow backward shifting of the stars), a new ruler now controls this circle. Draco's stars were still circumpolar in about 5000 BCE, but by 1100 BCE control, after passing through an empty "mouth," moved toward the stars of the Wagons (the Dippers).

By this late time, dragons were being killed, thrown from heaven, or driven underground to lurk in caverns under castles and churches. Odin, himself, singing his eighteen rune songs, taunts the dragon (Straystinger). However, dragons were still important enough that some rulers continued to identify with them.*

*King Arthur's father, for instance, adopted the name "head dragon," the Pendragons.

15. Algiz

Elk or Elk Sedge

Variants: Elhaz

You are my refuge and shield [. . .] Hold me up and I shall be safe.

"Psalm 119" (fifteenth Hebrew letter, samekh)

ALGIZ, THE HORNED ELK GODS

The fifteenth rune, Algiz, (or Elhaz) is translated both as elk and as "elk sedge." The word elk derives from the Latin Alcis, the name of ancient Germanic twin gods[1] who once traveled as horned stags. Their name, Alcis (Algiz) suggests they were elk-shaped gods.

Fig. 32. Drawing of Sedge with its horns.
UC Integrated Pest Management Program.

Fig. 33. Horned god, Enkomi,
12th century BCE.
Photo by Gerhard Haubold.

Long before they became devils, many ancient gods, like the protective sedge and the god Enkomi shown in figures 32 and 33, wore horns. Horned gods have offered protection and fertility to the land since Paleolithic times. Eventually, agriculture developed, and the symbol depicting the fifteenth rune ᛉ came to represent the horned barley. Derived from an older magic, the journey of John Barleycorn is a path followed by older shamans towards the light.

Barley dies to feed his people every year, and as a shield of protection, he offers a way of making peace: "Barley, a term used in games of children when a truce is demanded."[2] The grave symbol giving peace and food shows barley sacrificed and hung upside down. This shield is now the modern peace symbol ☮.*

PROTECTIVE WEAPONS

> The *Eolh-secg [elk sedge]* is mostly to be found in a marsh; it grows in the water and makes a ghastly wound, covering with blood every warrior who touches it.
>
> OLD ENGLISH RUNE POEM

In the mysteries of mathematics, there is a relationship between the third, and fifteenth symbols: both three and fifteen are triangular numbers. The triangular shape of the sedge's stem echoes the triangular third rune Thurisaz (thorn) ᚦ. Sedge spikes, unlike the round stems of reeds and grasses, emerge in whirls of three from their triangular stems. Like Mars' iron weapons associated with the third symbol, the razer-sharp leaves of the sedge (also known as saw grass) draw blood from the unwary traveler. As I know from personal experience, each blade of this grass has cutting teeth.

SEASONS AND CYCLES OF PLANETS

The numbers three and fifteen can also be found in astronomy where the cycles of the planets enrich fifteen's story. The potent bull of the moon takes thirty days to travel around the sky, becoming brightest during the three days surrounding the fifteenth.

The moon, Saturn, and Mars are among the various names for the god responsible for Earth's fertility. The journey of red Mars around the zodiac takes fifteen years, and once every fifteen years Mars appears particularly bright. Saturn is also brilliant every fifteen years, when it is halfway through a journey of thirty years around the sky.[3]

---

*Designed by Gerald Holtom, 1958.

NIGHT BRINGING ON DAY

> *The fifteenth I know: How Great Sage (Thiodrearer) the dwarf chanted before Delling's doors; he chanted strength into the Anses, and victory to the Elves, wisdom to the God of Counsel (Hropta-tyr).*
>
> VIGFUSSON, *HAVAMAL*

> [. . .] Instead of reckoning by days as we do, they reckon by nights, and in this manner fix both their ordinary and their legal appointments. Night, they regard as bringing on day.[4]

> Norfi or Narfi [. . .] had a daughter called Night [. . .] Her last husband was called Delling [Dawn] and together they had a son called Day. Odin took Night and Day and gave them a horse and chariot each to ride through the sky with.[5]

We have almost finished our journey through the dark Underworld. After fifteen steps into the heart of the Mystery, we have been measured and judged and have settled our debts. Only the pure of heart can finish the path but with the power of the next rune, we finally emerge into the light of day. We now stand at the gates of dawn. We meet the sun of Night and Dawn, Day's bright victory, arriving as the sixteenth rune.

16. Sowilo

Sun

Variants: Sowelo, Sigel (victory), or Sól (ᛊ, ᛌ)

Men do not live once in order to vanish forever. They live several lives in different places but not always in this world, and between each life there is a veil of shadows.

Ramses Seleem,
Illustrated Egyptian Book of the Dead

THE VEILS BETWEEN THE WORLDS

According to René Derolez, a gloss on the sun rune reads, "Sigel id est velum."[1] A velum is a thin veil, and this rune gloss may refer to the veil between the worlds. This veil now parts to let Mystery's Child, hidden fifteen deep steps into the Underworld, emerge into the sun of the sixteenth rune (eleventh in the Younger Futhark).

The sixteenth Phoenician letter Ayin (eye) o, is the eye through which the returning Sun slips back into the (material) world of his Mother. The shape came to represent the zero, the secretive cipher. Originally the ancient world avoided zeros since a god could never create

Fig. 34. Ouroboros drawing from a copy of a late medieval Byzantine Greek alchemical manuscript.

Drawing by Theodoros Pelecanos of Corfu, 1478. In Fol. 279 of *Codex Parisinus Graecus* 2327. Photo courtesy of Carlos Adanero.

a "no-thing." Finally arriving in the west from India via the Muslims, zero as the ouroboros—the sigel or sigil (symbol) of the snake eating its tail shown above—began to cycle endlessly through the opening eye. Each time this pupil of his Mother's eye returns, he brings increase to the mortal world. Ancient earth magic promised peace and wealth still measured into sixteen golden (troy) ounces, Denying the usual diminution of division, zero rather than being a "no-thing" always promises endless wealth: 1/0 = infinity.

O is also the eye of the needle which the camel representing the third Phoenician symbol, Gimel, can slip through, but only after sharing his wealth. Jews, like ancient Vikings, recognized there is more to life than hoarding gold. The alphabet poem of Psalm 119:127 says of Ayin, "More than gold and precious stones [. . .] I love thy commandments above gold, yea above fine gold." Gold, of course, loves only itself.

Mothers of Sixteen

Sixteen is the proper age for young virgins to bear their golden children. Ain/Ayin is an eye of the Hebrew sun. The Celtic sun goddess Aine, as mother-to-be, "appears in the word ain, meaning in my womb."[2] She sits on Ireland's birth chair in August to give birth to the gold of summer grain. An ancient chant invokes her:

> Erce, Erce, Erce, Mother of Earth! May the All-Wielder, Ever Lord grant thee. Acres a-waxing, upwards a-growing Pregnant [with corn] and plenteous in strength; Hosts of [grain] shafts and of glittering plants! Of broad barley the blossoms And of white wheat ears waxing, Of the whole earth the harvest![3]

Annapurna (full of food) of India is another young goddess of wealth, and Anna mothered Mary who delivered her son when she was sixteen. Lovely goddess Tara, born from a tear fallen from the eye of the Buddha of Compassion, is yet another maiden of sixteen.

Travel by Sun

> *Sigel (sun) is ever a joy in the hopes of seafarers when they journey away over the fishes' bath.*
>
> OLD ENGLISH RUNE POEM

In addition to the alchemical secrets of illumination, runes hide technical information among their number magic. As noted in the quote above, how to travel accurately when the sun is hidden from view is one such secret. In the days before the magnetic compass, when traveling over the sea or grassy steppes, you might travel by rope. This involved trailing a long rope behind you and trying to keep it straight to maintain the ship or wagon on a constant course. The safer way was to follow the direction of the sun by day and the stars by night. However, when these celestial bodies were hidden by fog or clouds, this was difficult if not impossible. For years, reports of Viking sunstones (*solarsteinn*) that made navigation possible even on cloudy days were considered myths. However, recently archeologists came across a sunstone from the Alderney shipwreck of 1592. It contained an Icelandic calcite spar thought to be the crystal used for navigation.

It is thought that sunstones were polarizing crystals, which could be used to locate the sun's rays: "In particular, at twilight when the sun is no longer observable being below the horizon, and the stars still not [yet] observable, this optical device could provide the mariners with an absolute reference in such situation."[4]

> *Sól (Sun) shield of the clouds and shining ray and destroyer of ice.*
>
> *Sól er skýja skjöldr ok skínandi röðull ok ísa aldrtregi. rota siklingr.*
> Glosses: *Rota* (wheel), *siklingr* (king)
>
> Old Icelandic Rune Poem

Sol is the Elder Futhark's 16th rune, Ice being Younger Futhark's 11th. Both the OIRP and ONRP moved the shining sun to 11th position once occupied by the Ice rune. The sun is, of course the destroyer of the Ice.

THE TURNING WHEEL

The sixteenth Elder Futhark rune is the victorious sun, but it is also related to the gloss *rota*, or "wheel." A kenning (poetical name) for the sun is the dwarf's wheel, and the four metalworking dwarves who stand in each of Earth's directions spin the wheel. (They made the shining necklace, the Brisingamen for Freya). By Germanic times alphabet magic had been adapted to the needs of warriors. The victory rune now also implied a sigel of war as well as the Wheel of Rebirth: "Sigrúnar (Victory-runes) learn if you long to win."[5]

Sixteen's promise of a warrior's victory might once have promised love. This charm apparently uses the sun rune to warm the heart of a young maid: "I know a sixteenth if I want to have all a clever woman's heart and love-play; I can turn the thoughts of the white-armed woman and change her mind completely."[6]

"Snake in the Eye" and the Ouroboros

Reincarnation on the Wheel returning the soul was never completely forgotten. Earlier I related the story of the Valkyrie Sigrdrifa (Brynhild) who was reborn, joining her love in the next life. Sigrdrifa was reborn as Cara, and her lover as Helgi as the ruler of the Hadding clan. Their son is Ragnar Hairy Britches (Lodbrok), and their grandson is the semi historical Viking, Sigurd Snake in the Eye (Sigurðr ormr í auga). Before their deaths, Brynhild and Sigurd had a beautiful daughter, Aslaug. Raised by peasants after her mother's death, Aslaug was blackened by tar and renamed Kraka (Crow) to hide her beauty.

Ragnar Lodbrok discovered Aslaug's radiance while she was bathing and married her. To prove she was indeed the noble granddaughter of Sigurd the dragon slayer, she said her son would be born with a snake in his eye. Her son, Sigurd Snake in the Eye, was so named because he was born with a mark in his left eye, an image of the ouroboros mentioned earlier encircling the pupil of his eye.[7]

Conclusion to the Second Aettir

We now end our travels through the second family of runes, Hel's Underworld. For those who journeyed past seven's ending, past the gate of the bright eighth rune into the labyrinth, the sixteenth rune returns us to the light.

The sixteenth charm is a place one can step off the Wheel, or like Sigrun return. When we reached the eleventh rune, we paused before continuing on our path through the Underworld. Now, before rising in the heavens, we again pause to catch our breath: "In many languages, there is a break after sixteen."[8]

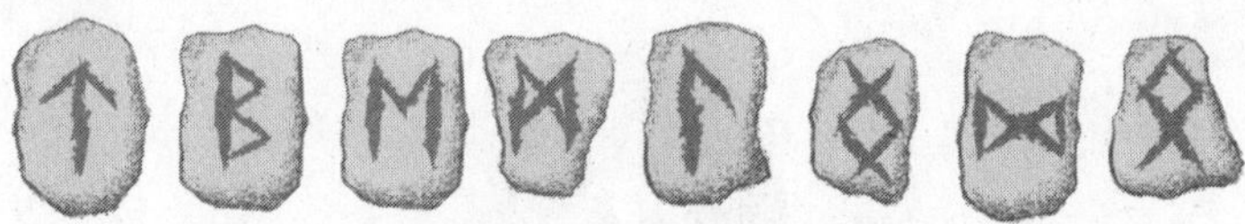

Third Aettir

Tir's Family

TIRS RUNES

Number	Name	Meaning
17	Tir, Tiuwaz, Tyr	God of the North Star, identified with Mars
18	Berkano, Beorc, or Bjarkan	Birch or Poplar
19	Ehwaz or Eh	Horse
20	Mannaz	Man
21	Laguz, Logr, or Laukaz	Water, lake, or leek
22	Ingwaz	Earth god, also known as Ingvi-Freyr
23	Dagaz	Day (sometimes placed as number 24)
24	Othala	Homeland or inheritance

We entered the wealth of Freyr's material earth via the first eight runes. Passing through the white (Wynn/Wunjo) gate of the eighth Phoenician letter, Heth, we then traveled the Underworld of Hel's family, returning to the light through the victorious sixteenth rune (Sowilo).

This last family of runes describes the heavens and further astronomical and mathematical secrets. It begins with Tiuwaz, once ruler of the stars turning over the north. The eighteenth and nineteenth runes have references to sun and moon cycles. After their orbits reconcile every nineteen years (Metonic cycle), the twentieth year heads a new cycle.

Because there are fewer patterns helping to illustrate the rune choices, I now include some information on the last four of the twenty-four letters of the Greek alphabet, which offer clues for understanding the final rune symbols.

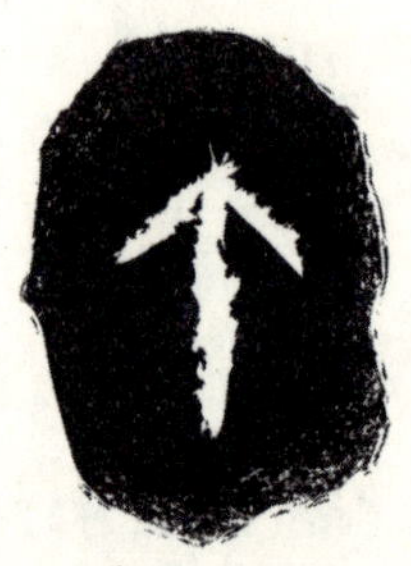

17. Tiuwaz

Guiding Star

Variants: *Tiwaz, Teiwaz, Tir, or Týr*

God of the North Star, identified with Mars

Týr is a one-handed god; often has the smith to blow.
Old Norwegian Rune Poem

Tir is a guiding star; well does it keep faith with princes; it is ever on its course over the mists of night and never fails.
Old English Rune Poem

COMMAND OF THE SKY

Tir (Tiwaz), owner of the seventeenth rune, is associated with law, the North Star, and Mars. His north-pointing arrow appears among the stars of Sirius/Orion. An imaginary line through the three stars of Orion's belt toward the horizon points roughly north toward the pole-star he once commanded. His arrow still points north on our maps.

As a guide for sailors or travelers over the flat steppes, the height of the star indicates the latitude. Keeping it at the same height over the shoulder sends one marching in a straight east-west direction. The North Star is almost directly overhead in the northern latitudes.

Tir was the Germanic High God before Odin replaced him as war leader. His name can be found in some of Odin's names: Hanga-tyr or Hropta-tyr. Tir (Tiwaz), cognate with Zeus and Deus, was the son of Earth, *tir* meaning "earth" in Celtic. After the ONRP and OIRP reduced the twenty-four Elder Futhark runes to sixteen, Tir appears as the twelfth rune, the position of the High King, our letter L (eL).

Opening the Mouth

The seventeenth Hebrew letter is Pe, meaning "mouth" or "command." As Psalm 119 states, "I opened my mouth and panted. For I longed for thy commandments."[1] All stars circling the pole star, Greeks, adapting the earlier alphabet used Pi π as their 17th letter, a symbol controlling the circumference of circles $C = 2\ \pi r$). After death, Egypt had a ritual of Opening the Mouth so the dead could enjoy eating and talking while ascending to the stars: "The little gadgets used for the Opening the Mouth were given the celestial shape of the Big Dipper [polestars]."[2]

The tool was made of star iron thrown from the sky: "My mouth is opened by Ptah [. . .] He looses the bonds of Set/Seth from my mouth."[3] This ceremony loosened the bonds of Set. Red Set, like Mars, (Seth) is another god of war. Associated with the third day (belonging to Tir and Mars), the bonds and bolts of Time are imposed when the world is seeded, is impregnated, on the third day of Genesis.

Mars and Magnetism

Seventeen represents victory in war. Rust-red, warring Mars, another name associated with Tir, rules the Iron Age: "In classical antiquity [number seventeen] appears in connection with warfare and heroism."[4] In the Bible, number seventeen symbolizes "overcoming the enemy and 'complete victory.' God overcame the [. . .] rebellious humans when he [flooded] the earth on the 17th of the second Hebrew month."[5]

Some iron ores are magnetic. Magnetic iron (magnetite) is a lodestone, which when suspended to turn freely acts as a compass, faithfully pointing north. Like the North Star once ruled by Draco, it guides travelers faithfully even when the stars are obscured.

This same magnetism empowered Odin's seventeenth rune charm, keeping his lover attracted: "The seventeenth I know: That the young maid shall never forsake me."[6] Made of the same iron running through a red-blooded lover's veins, the lodestone was carried by prostitutes in ancient Europe, fed water and iron on Fridays by Mexicans, and formed into statues of lovers. In Greece, a lodestone goddess was set free once a year to rush toward her lover made of iron.[7]

REMEMBERING THE PRECESSION.

To understand Tir's downfall, we must revisit the precession of the equinoxes. The slight wobble of Earth on its axis results in the pole-stars slowly shifting from their original position. The removal of the dragon—Draco—from his position of power and his replacement by the stars of the Wagons (the Dippers), is one result. As the deposed star slips away, a ravenous mouth opens until a new star captures the pole. The center does not hold, until a new Nail of the North arrives. The stars rising in spring also slowly shift backward. Passing through the zodiac ages of Taurus and Aries, we are now in Pisces moving toward the unsettled Age of Aquarius.

CAPTURING THE MOUTH

> *Týr—god with one hand and leavings of the wolf and prince of temples.*
>
> *Týr er einhendr áss ok ulfs leifar ok hofa hilmir. Mars tiggi.*
> Glosses: Mars, *tiggi* (king)
>
> Old Icelandic Rune Poem

In the northern tradition, Tir captured the mouth of the wolf threatening to consume the world. Tir was a righteous god, a just god who never broke his word . . . until he did. When Fenrir, a violent wolf, threatened

Fig. 35. Tir with his hand in Fenrir's mouth.
Illustration by John Bauer, 1911.

the stability of the Norse world, the gods convinced the wolf to submit to being bound as a test of his power. Promising to release him, Tir held his hand in the wolf's mouth as guarantee. When he broke his word, the wolf bit off his hand at the "wolf joint" (wrist). Escaping his bonds on the day of Ragnarok, the wolf will kill the oath breaker Odin. Garm, the dog of Hel, will kill Tir: "Now Garm bays loudly before Gnipa-cave. The fetter will break, and the ravener (wolf run) free."[8]

18. Berkan

Birch or Poplar

Variants: *Beorc, Björk, Berkano, or Bjarkan*

BIRCH BARK

Berc id est cortex

SIXTEENTH-CENTURY GLOSS
ON THE BIRCH RUNE[1]

Writing is not usually associated with the eighteenth rune, Berkano (birch), but the gloss above was added when the old knowledge of runes was disappearing. The word *cortex* originated from Proto-Indo-European word *ker* or *sker*, meaning "to cut." By the 1650s it had come to mean "outer-shell, husk [. . .] some part or structure resembling bark or rind."[2]

Paper birch has long been used for writing (see figure on the next page). Marks scratched on the bark's white surface show as nicely as on a modern sheet of paper. The first message written in an Irish script known as ogham was scratched onto birch bark. It warned that the queen might be carried off to the Underworld. In that script, Beith (birch) is the first letter, a position associated with the origins of writing.

Fig. 36. Birch-bark letter no. 202, Russian child's spelling lessons circa 1240–1260.

Uploaded image courtesy of Nikola Smolenski.

Birch and the Midwife Moon

> *Thou must know,*
> *if thou wilt help to deliver a woman of a child.*
> *Grave them on the palm of the hand, and clasp it on the wrist,*
> *and cry upon the Fairies [disir] for help.*
>
> "Sigrdrifumal," in *Corpus Poeticum Boreale*,
> Vigfusson and Powell trans.

The quote above refers to *bjargrúnar*, or "birth runes" being engraved on the palms of midwives' hands. Eighteen is a number associated with birth and midwife moons. Birch, Lady of the Woods, represents new beginnings; baby's cradles were made from its wood. According to Ralph Elliot in *Runes*, birch has a traditional association with the awakening in spring, fertility, and birth.[3] As an aid to the midwife, number eighteen, like thirteen, reflects the moon's cycles, and the moon has a long connection with midwives.

> *(Bjarkan) Birch leafy twig and little tree and fresh young shrub.*
>
> *Bjarkan er laufgat lim ok lítit tré ok ungsamligr viðr. abies buðlungr.*
> Glosses: *Abies* (fir), *buðlungr* (poet or king)
>
> OLD ICELANDIC RUNE POEM

The Younger Futhark moved Berkano to the thirteenth position, reflecting this association with moon cycles, and the OIRP has it glossed with "fir," a tree of life like the birch. Fir needles were burned at childbirth to bless and protect the mother and baby. As the thirteenth rune of the Younger Futhark, Berkano still appears at a position associated with moons and childbirth.

THE MOON'S EIGHTEEN YEAR CYCLES

Our wandering moon has an 18-year cycle. The Saros cycle describes a period occurring every 18 years and eleven days when the sun and moon nodes (where the moon crosses the ecliptic) line up and an eclipse can occur. Every three cycles (54 years) the eclipse occurs in the same zodiac sign. There is another lunar cycle of 18.6 years when the moon is closest to Earth, appearing especially large in the sky. The appearance of this super moon is especially impressive.

THE FIRES OF LOKI

> *(The poplar) bears no fruit; yet without seed it brings forth suckers,*
> *for it is generated from its leaves.*
> *Splendid are its branches and gloriously adorned*
> *its lofty crown which reaches to the skies.*
>
> OLD ENGLISH RUNE POEM

The OERP describes a tree that is usually translated as "poplar" rather than birch. The *Populus* family includes aspens, which are often confused with birch. Unlike the birch, they produce suckers and "reproduce asexually [that is, without seed] after fire by sprouting from the basal buds [. . .] whose aboveground tissues are killed by fire."[4]

This hints at the eighteenth rune's association with the trickster Loki, who is literally "wildfire." Beorc is generated from leaves; hermaphrodite Loki was generated from Laufey (full of leaves).

> *Bjarkan (Birch) has the greenest leaves of any shrub; Loki was fortunate in his deceit.*
>
> Old Norwegian Rune Poem

Multi-sexual Loki both fathered and mothered his children among whom are Hel, the Fenrir wolf, the Midgard Serpent, and Odin's eight-legged horse.

19. Ehwaz

Horse

Variant: Eh

(Horse) is a joy to princes in the presence of warriors. A steed in the pride of its hoofs, when rich men on horseback bandy words about it; and it is ever a source of comfort to the restless.

Old English Rune Poem

THE GOLDEN NUMBER OF THE SUN

Nineteen is a golden number associated with the sun and the Metonic cycle—a period of nineteen years, at the end of which the phases of the sun begin to occur in the same order and on the same days as in the previous cycle. Bronze Age people may have been aware of the nineteen-year cycle at an early period as the images that follow suggest.

The great sun might sail the sky in a boat. Notice that nineteen prongs appear on the boat transporting the sun wheel shown on page 139. In the North, the sun and moon were also driven by horses. Ehwaz (horse) is the nineteenth rune in the Elder Futhark.

Every nineteen years, the cycles of the sun, moon, and Mercury realign. The nineteenth Phoenician/Hebrew letter is *Qopf,* which is translated as "monkey." The alphabet arising in Egypt associated

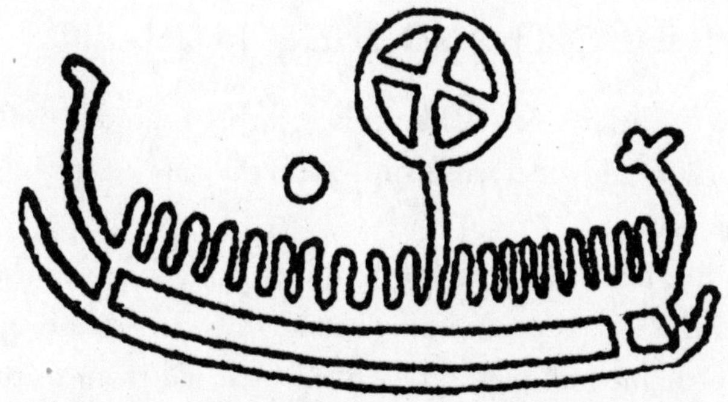

Fig. 37. Sun boat, Bronze Age, Scandinavia, c. 3000 BCE.

From Gimbutas, *The Language of the Goddess*, 249.

monkeys with the sun. At the time of Creation, baboons were formed to praise each rising sun: "I have sung and praised the sun disc. I have joined the baboons."[1]

Runic calendars were developed based on the nineteen-year-long Metonic cycle, and many were carved onto staves. The oldest calendar known is the Nykoping staff, believed to date from the thirteenth century. The rune staff, or runic almanac, began with the first full moon after the winter solstice, and the sixteen runes of the Younger Futhark represent the first sixteen years of the cycle. Three special runes were created to complete the nineteen years needed to represent the sun's Metonic cycle. They were Arlaug (seventeen), Tvimadur (eighteen), and Belgthor (nineteen),[2] which are shown below. Note that Belgthor is very similar to the symbol for the nineteenth Phoenician letter Qopf. The new moon on the eighteenth year of each cycle would fall on all the dates marked with Tvimadur.

Fig. 38a. Arlaug (seventeen).

Fig. 38b. Tvimadur (eighteen).

Fig. 38c. Belgthor (nineteen).

Uploaded by Bencoland.

THE HORSE AND THE SUN CHARIOT

By the time of the creation of the runes, rather than the sun sailing in a boat, a horse as the nineteenth rune pulls the chariot carrying the sun through the sky:

The figure below is of "a horse drawing a solar disc in a chariot. One side of the disc is gold and light and the other side is bronze and dark [. . .] Ornamental units on each side, has led them to the conclusion that the light side depicts a 366-day solar calendar, and the dark side depicts a 354-day lunar calendar."[3]

> There was a person whose name was Mundilfari who had two children [. . .] he called the son Mani (moon) and his daughter Sol (sun) [. . .] But the gods got angry [. . .] and took the brother and sister [. . .] and made Sol drive the horses that drew the chariot of the sun [. . .] Mani guides the course of the moon.[4]

Fig. 39. Trundholm sun chariot drawn by horse, Denmark, c. 1400 BCE.

National Museum of Denmark.

Although couched in myth and poetry, it is obvious these far-ranging Norsemen were aware of the cycles of the sun, moon, and stars: "How shall the sun be referred to? By calling it daughter of Munilfaeri, sister of Moon, wife of Glen, fire of sky and air."[5] The Sun's husband, Glenr, is translates as "an opening in the clouds," and Mundilfaeri, father of the Sun and Moon (Mani), literally moves as a "period of time."

At the end of the Norse world at Ragnarok, on the Day of the Wolf, the sun joins the gods in death:

> *How will there still be a Sun when the Wolf has eaten*
> *[this one]?*
> *The sun will have a daughter before Fenrir [the wolf]*
> *eats her.*
> *And that young sun will travel on her mother's path*
> *when the gods have all died."*
>
> "Vafthruthnismal,"
> in *The Poetic Edda*,
> Crawford, trans., 57

20. Mannaz

Man

Variants: Maðr or Mathr (ᛘ)

Maðr (Man) is an augmentation of the dust; Great is the claw of the hawk.

Old Norwegian Rune Poem

(Man) is the joy of man and the increase of dust and the adornment of ships.

Maðr er manns gaman ok moldar auki ok skipa skreytir. homo mildingr.
Glosses: *Homo* (man), *mildingr* (generous one)

Old Icelandic Rune Poem,
Thorsson trans.

DEATH AND REBIRTH

Mannaz, or Man, is the twentieth rune in the Elder Futhark. It is the fourteenth symbol in the Younger Futhark. When the Younger Futhark reduced the twenty-four runes to sixteen, the symbolic placement of the runes was maintained. Described above, Man, the adornment of ships, is placed in the position of the returning king emerging from his mother's ship over the waters of the thirteenth Phoenician/ Hebrew letter Mem (water). Entering the material world, the world of time and death, he will increase the dust when his body returns to earth once again.

> *Man is in his mirth dear to his kinsman; although each*
> *shall depart from the other; for the lord wants to commit,*
> *by his decree, that frail flesh to the earth.*
>
> Old English Rune Poem, Thorsson trans.

Once Man enters the world of Time, he enters the world of Death. The Man rune, like barley or the deadly Yew rune, turned upside down ᛦ indicated death on some early documents. But as oft repeated, Egypt's Mystery traditions transmitted by the Phoenicians hid the promise of rebirth.

THE HEAD OF A NEW CYCLE

Rising again after the finality of the nineteen-year sun cycle, a new beginning arrives with each twentieth year. The twentieth Phoenician letter, Ros, literally means the "head" of each new cycle. Although runes chose their letter shapes from their own hoard of images, the twentieth Phoenician letter (Ros/head) 𐤓 is similar to the shape used for the thorn, or the "prick," of the third rune ᚦ. With three's charm, the world of Time begins when lightning arrows seed Earth and dry her red waters with impregnation. The vernal equinox began each new year in ancient Mesopotamia in the third month of March, and the modern zodiac cycle still begins with arrow-shooting Aries (Mars) in the same month.

Astronomy affected the placement of many early alphabet symbols, and every twenty years a grand conjunction occurs when Saturn, lord of time, and kingly Jupiter shine together in the sky. Occasionally, Mars joins the grand group. The ancient world considered this conjunction to signal important events, including disasters and death.

21. Laguz

Lake or Leek

Variants: Lögr (water) or Laukaz

Lögr: Water is eddying stream and broad geysir and land of the fish.

Lögr er vellanda vatn ok viðr ketill ok glömmungr grund. lacus lofðungr.
Glosses: *Lacus* (lake), *lofðungr* (king)

Old Icelandic Rune Poem

THE WATERY LAKE RUNE

The Laguz (water) rune, number twenty-one in the Elder Futhark and fifteen in the Younger, is similar in shape to the third Phoenician letter Gimel: 𐤂.*

As a number, twenty-one, the sum of the first six natural numbers is another triangular number (1 + 2 + 3 + 4 + 5 + 6 = 21).†

*While it is unlikely that runes developed directly from ancient Phoenician/Hebrew alphabet, the qualities of the twenty-first symbol seem to reflect those of the third: 2 + 1 = 3.

†See the explanation in the Thurisaz rune chapter.

The Futhark's placement of a Sedge as 15th rune may result from its being another triangular number. The horned Elk-sedge, #15 of the Elder Futhark, has a triangular stem; reed stems being round. Measurements of 5 + 5 + 5 = 15 also create equilateral triangles. Described above, the numbers three, six, ten, and fifteen are all triangular numbers and as such are associated with fertility and the generation of new life (or in 10's case, new numbers).

The third rune is a thorn with all a prick's phallic connotations. Six is the marriage of midsummer's honeymoon producing kin. Ten, of course, generates all numbers following her (10 + 1, 10 + 2, and so on). The fifteenth Phoenician letter is Samekh, the old devil some claim impregnated Eve with her first son, Cain, and the fifteenth rune in the Younger Futhark (Algiz) represents the horned elk, the king of the forest. Here, the gloss of *lofðungr* (king) may refer to the potency of the phallic symbol since kings are notorious for passing on copies of their genes among multiple families. Various gods manifested as the virile elk including the fertile Freyr.

Greeks eventually placed the phallic phi Φ as the twenty-first out of their twenty-four letters rather than leaving it in its original nineteenth position (which became their *Q*). In Lacanian algebra Φ stands for the phallus–Φ stands in for castration.[1]

Leeks and Fertility

Laguz, sometimes translated as "leek," a member of the onion family which has been associated with increased testosterone in men. The Leek hypothesis is based on early inscriptions like those found on

Fig. 40. Leek emerging from its hairy nest.
Photo by Bjorn Konig.

the Bülach fibula, a disk-like brooch found in Switzerland, where the rune is thought to abbreviate *laukaz*. The inscription, written in Elder Futhark runes, begs, "[I, your] lover with the penis, you with the vulva: receive me; leek! penis! leek! penis!"[2]

THE LEEK AND THE VOLSUNGAS

The existing poems for this rune seem to bypass the potency of the leek's symbolism, but the rune as Leek has a connection to the Wulfing family of Volsi: Sigurd's Volsungas. It has been suggested that Völsung and his family evoked the fertility of a stallion.[3]

The "Völsa þáttr," a short story from the Óláfs saga in the Flateyjarbok, gives a stallion's preserved phallus being worshipped in a ritual that named Volsi. A woman wrapped the penis in linen and covered it with leeks whereby it continued to grow: "By the power of the devil the thing grew and became so strong, that it could stand upright by the old woman, when she wanted it to." After the ritual one of the characters observes, "You're distended, Volsi, and pricked up. Endowed by linen and supported by leeks."[4]

Cursed Gold and Waterfalls

> *Lögr: A waterfall is a river which falls from a mountainside;*
> *but ornaments are of gold.*
>
> OLD NORWEGIAN RUNE POEM

Gold and water are also associated with Laguz, or Logr. As we've seen throughout our journey through the runes, a cursed gold wreaks havoc and causes the deaths of all who possess it. The river gold was originally stolen from a dwarf named Andvari, who often took the form of a fish living under a waterfall (Logr). Among his vast golden treasures was a ring, the Andvaranaut. The trickster Loki captured Andvari in a net borrowed from Ran, goddess of the sea. Forced to give up his gold as ransom, the dwarf cursed the ring, promising everyone who owned it would die.

Fig. 41. Drävle runestone, showing the dwarf on left holding his ring.
Photo courtesy of Bengt A. Lundberg/Riksantikvarieämbetet.

When Loki killed Fafnir's brother, Ótr (who had shapeshifted into an otter), he was forced to give up all the gold to pay the debt (wergeld) to Ótr's father. Fafnir then turned himself into a dragon, killing his father to steal the gold. Continuing the curse, his brother Regin convinced the Volsung Sigurd to kill Fafnir for the gold (see the chapter on the fifth rune, Raido). Warned by birds that Regin planned to kill him as well, Sigurd then killed Regin, took the sword, and loaded the gold on his horse. In time, the ring's curse killed him as well.

> *Lagu: The ocean seems interminable to men, if they venture on the rolling bark and the waves of the sea terrify them and the courser of the deep heed not its bridle.*
>
> Old English Rune Poem

The net that captured the original owner of the cursed gold belonged to Ran, goddess of the sea. In the event their deep-sea coursers are sunk under stormy waves, northern sailors carry small bits of gold to give Ran and her spouse, Aegir, when they join them under the water.

Rán had that net wherein she was wont to catch all men who go upon the sea. Now this tale is to show [. . .] that gold is called Fire or Light or Brightness of Ægir, of Rán, or of Ægir's daughters; and now such use is made of these metaphors that gold is called Fire of the Sea, and of all names of the sea, even as Ægir or Rán, had names associated with the sea. Therefore gold is now called Fire of Waters or of Rivers, and of all river names.[5]

22. INGWAZ

EARTH GOD

Variants: *Inguz, Ing, or Ingvi-Freyr* (ᛜ, ᛝ)

> *[Ing] was first seen by men among the East-Danes, til, followed by his car, he departed eastwards over the waves. So the Heardingas named the hero.*
>
> OLD ENGLISH RUNE POEM

SATURN'S AVATAR

The rune ᛝ representing Ingvi is an alchemy symbol for lead, a material associated with Saturn. The earth god Ingvi-Freyr's father Njordr, one of the Vanir gods, is recognized as an avatar of Saturn. Saturn's astronomy symbol ♄ also represents an alchemist's lead. Orion, once known as Saturnus, lies near the river of the Milky Way by Gemini and Taurus.

DYNASTIES AND DESCENDENTS

Many royal dynasties claimed gods as ancestors. Among these were the kings of Sweden (the East-Danes) known as the Ynglings. Their ancestor was Ingvi-Freyr (Frodi), the ruler of a lost Golden Age once responsible for his Earth's fertility. When he died, his body was wheeled around in a wagon while his escort collected tribute from worshippers for years before admitting he was dead. In time he was laid in a burial mound with a door through which gifts of gold, silver, and copper were placed: "Frodi, who the Danes would have wished to live long, they bore long through their lands when he was dead. The great chief's body, with this turf heaped above it, earth covers under the lucid sky."[1]

KINGS AND CORN BRING ABUNDANCE AND PROTECTION

Another ancestor bringing abundance to his land is the Danish king Scyld (Scyldings is another name for the Danes). Scyld, the Sheaf Child, arrived in a boat and eventually grew into a powerful king. Similar traditions tell of Sceaf (Sheave) coming over the sea with a sheaf of corn (grain), bringing wealth to the land.

The "Havamal" claims that an ear of corn protects against witchcraft. ". . . when ale thou quaffest, call upon earth's might—'tis earth drinks in the floods. Earth prevails o'er drink, but fire o'er sickness, the oak o'er binding, the earcorn o'er witchcraft."[2]

While an ear or sheaf of corn does not appear in any existing stories of the Haddings, (the Heardingas mentioned in the OERP above) it appears in the "Lay of Gudrun." In the previous chapter on Laguz, I described the gold ring cursed by the dwarf from whom his gold had been stolen. The ring and gold were taken from the dragon Fafnir by Sigurd, who gave the ring to Sigrdrifa (Brynhild) promising her marriage. Given a draft of forgetfulness, he was tricked into marrying Gudrun. When Gudrun's brothers kill Sigurd, Brynhild "stabs herself, has a stately pyre and bale-fire made, and is burnt thereon with Sigurd's body." After her death, she rides down the path to Hell in her chariot to join her lover in the grave.[3]

Gudrun is then forced to marry Attila the Hun, who kills her brothers but is unable to seize the gold. Her brothers are revenged by

Gudrun, but after killing Attila, she joins her husband on the funeral pyre. Before her marriage, she was given a potion by her mother that contained several runes and among them Haddingland's unshorn ear of corn, possibly a magic Vandal rune:

> *In the cup were runes of every kind,*
> *Written and reddened, I could not read them;*
> *A heather-fish from the Haddings' land,*
> *An ear uncut, and the entrails of beasts.*
>
> "THE SECOND LAY OF GUDRUN,"
> HENRY ADAMS BELLOWS TRANS.

A "heather-fish" is another name for the lindworm, which is a gold-loving dragon like Fafnir. An "ear uncut" describes the sheaf of corn (wheat or grain) bringing good fortune and abundance to the land while protecting against evil witchcraft.

Ynglings and the Lindworm

Thora, the first wife of Yngling Ragnar Hairy Britches, kept a small lindworm that eventually grew to a great size, threatening her home. Ragnar put on hairy britches to protect himself from the worm's poison and killed it.

After Thora died, Ragnar married the daughter of dragon slayer Sigurd and Brynhild. She was the beautiful Aslaug who had been fostered by peasants. They covered her with soot and tar to hide her beauty, calling her Kraka (crow). Ragnar Hairy Britches, after seeing her true beauty during her bath, took her to wife.

The Hardings

We return once again to the story of Sigrun and her lover Helgi Hundingsbane, who were reborn as Cara and Helgi Haddingjaskati, the ruler of the Haddings.

The Heardingas, or Haddings, were the royal dynasty of the Vandals. They possibly possessed the magic unshorn ear of corn rune of Haddingland given to Gudrun in the story told previously). Famous for sacking Rome (455 CE), they "may have worshipped Ing while they were in south Sweden, and carried his cult to Denmark, and further east (over the waves) when they migrated from Scandinavia."[4] Followers of Ing acquired the name Yngling. Harding is a name still used for people from west Norway:

> The Harding name [may be linked to two areas] one from Norway—the Hardanger Fjord, where people are still called "Hardings" or "Hardinger." [. . .] The other as Danish/Angle hordes [recorded in the Old English Rune Poem as the] Germanic tribe Heardingas. Both groups may have originated from [. . .] the Jutland peninsula, who under pressure of expanding groups around them moved to [the] Horderland-Hardanger area [. . .] In Icelandic literature they are the "Haddings" and their legendary leader Hadding is protected by both Thor and Odin.[5]

When orphaned, Hadding was fostered by giants. His foster sister Harthgrepa asked him to be her lover. When he answered, her giant body was too large for the embraces of a mortal, and she said:

> Be not moved by my unwonted look of size. For my substance is sometimes thinner, sometimes ampler; now meagre, now abundant; and I alter and change at my pleasure the condition of my body, which is at one time shriveled up and at another time expanded: now my tallness rises to the heavens, and now I settle down into a human being, under a more bounded shape.[6]

When he returned home, she came with him. Spending a night in a house whose host had just died, Harthgrepa practicing rune magic made Hadding put a stick carved with spells under the corpse's tongue. Compelled to speak, the corpse cursed them, predicting their deaths. Under Odin's patronage, Hadding became the first king of Denmark. Years later, after a friend drowned in a vat of ale he "ends his life by suicide, and hangs himself publicly, as if making a voluntary sacrifice to Odin."[7]

The OERP overtly links Ingvi and Hadding: Hadding is the first Danish king, and Ing was "first seen by men among the East-Danes." Hadding was important enough that after death he was personally escorted on the back of Odin's eight-legged horse "over land and sea until they came to the god's dwelling."[8]

23. DAGAZ

DAY

Variant: Dæg

Dæg (Day) the glorious light of the Creator, is sent by the Lord; it is beloved of men, a source of hope and happiness to rich and poor, and of service to all.

OLD ENGLISH RUNE POEM

PSYCHE'S STORY

Dagaz's (Day's) emerging butterfly ᛞ is sometimes placed as the twenty-fourth rune, but more often as the twenty-third symbol. The Greeks eventually placed Psyche's (butterfly) letter *psi* as their 23rd letter. A late tale, Psyche's story is another connected with the Mystery journey into and return from the dark. Psyche must never see her lover by day. Like a sleeping butterfly, she entered the dark cocoon of the Underworld to perform tasks mandated by a goddess before returning to the light of Day and to her lover, Cupid.

Psyche was the youngest of three daughters of an unidentified king of Miletus. The Milesians, the first people to use the alphabet as numbers in their practice of gematria, claimed the Phoenician Cadmus as an ancestor.

Fig. 42. Psyche sculpture by Pietro Tenerani, 1819.

Uploaded by Paolobon140.

24. Othala

Homeland or Inheritance

Variants: *Ethel or Othila*

> *Ethel [homeland] is very dear to every man if he can enjoy there in his house whatever is right and proper in constant prosperity.*
>
> Old English Rune Poem

THE FINAL SYMBOLS

The Classical Greeks, expanding their alphabet to twenty-four letters, ended with the womb of Omega. It derives from their sixteenth letter Omicron ("little O") where other alphabets place the eye of the sun. The Greek alphabet is now bookended by the Alpha and Omega: "I am Alpha and Omega, the beginning and the end, the first and the last."[1]

The Younger Futhark of sixteen runes ends with Yr, the deadly yew, the corpse augmenting the earth. The Anglo-Saxon Runes, developed after Christian times, were expanded, adding four more symbols beyond the twenty-four runes of the Elder Futhark. In time, their rune list ended with the finality of the grave. The promise of resurrection has been lost; the covenant once given by the ancient Earth Mother to her seed was broken.

But the Phoenician/Hebrew alphabet and the Elder Futhark promised an escape from death and a return to life and the light. The last Phoenician/Hebrew letter, Tav, is written with a plus sign of a good return or with an *X* promising a multiplication of lives, promising the Angel of Death will pass over. The Elder Futhark, the runes which we have been highlighting throughout our journey, ended with the promise of a material, earthy homeland.

At the end of time, described variously as Ragnarok/Day of the Wolf, Kali Yuga, and the Great Flood, comes the end of each precession cycle. The old world dies, but a new green world emerges. Othala, the last of the twenty-four runes in the Elder Futhark, stood for a welcoming homeland. On the Day of the Wolf, the Norse world was destroyed, but the homeland endured. The Voluspa remembers the future:

> *She sees coming up a second time,*
> *Earth from the ocean, eternally green.*
> *The waterfalls plunge, an eagle soars above them,*
> *Over the mountain hunting fish.*
>
> "The Seer's Prophecy,"
> (Voluspa) from *The Poetic Edda*,
> Larrington trans.

Finale

We began our story in the black lands of Egypt. There, a genius or perhaps a few brilliant scholars adapted a few sacred letter images, hieroglyphs, renaming them in a Semitic language known as Canaanite and Old Hebrew. Along with this new script, they encrypted a spell promising a return to the light. In Egypt, images representing the spell of the Coming Forth by Day were first painted on the tombs of pharaohs. Eventually high-ranking officials and finally less elevated persons who could afford the expense acquired the images promising a return after death.

After the Semitic alphabet languished unused for a thousand years, a "man from the East" stole it and carried it to the lands around the Great Green Sea of the Mediterranean. The Mystery of a return to life among its symbols, the Greeks renamed the Canaanites Phoenicians after the Phoenix, the firebird who rises reborn from the ashes of destruction. After they gifted their alphabet to the Greeks, it became known as Phoenician. As the new alphabet traveled, some lucky few were initiated into the Mysteries of rebirth hidden among the images. Faithfully following the pattern of the older spell, runes used objects from their own traditions to represent the letters. Thus, they maintained both the order of the original alphabet and the purity of the mysterious spell it possessed.

In this book, we have considered the Norse rune alphabet, specifically the twenty-four runes of the Elder Futhark that described the Mystery of a return to an inherited home as their last chapter, Othala.

But over time, this return became an old wife's tale: the welcoming homeland of the early runes was transmuted into the deadly Yew of the Younger Futhark and with the passage of time the old ways were lost and forgotten.

As I believe I have shown throughout this book, the runes contain a mnemonic device: a spell, a Mystery, that has been preserved in the runic poems and medieval manuscripts. By following the hints laid out in Norse sagas and old memories, it is possible to reconstruct the original intent of the early rune masters who once promised to Fin-Again—Begin-Again.

Notes

INTRODUCTION. THE MAGIC OF RUNES: A BRIEF HISTORY OF THE FIRST ALPHABET

1. Tacitus, *The Complete Works of Tacitus.*
2. Koller, "The Alphabet: The First Thousand Years."
3. Herodotus, *The History of Herodotus.*
4. Nonnus, *Nonnus Dionysiaca*, 339.
5. Waal, "Mother or Sister? Rethinking the Origins of the Greek Alphabet and Its Relation to the Other 'Western' Alphabets."
6. Sturluson, *Edda*, Faulkes, trans., 3.
7. "Archaeological Evidence from Bulgaria Shows That Ancient Thrace Was Part of the Cretan-Mycenaean Culture," Novo Scriptorium.
8. Sanders, *The Invention of Hebrew*, 107.

RUNES: A MYTHIC HISTORY

1. Derolez, *Runica Manuscripta: The English Tradition*, xv.
2. Sturluson, *The Yglinga Saga,* Laing, trans.
3. Davidson, *Scandinavian Mythology*, 82.
4. Sturluson, "Skaldskapamal," in *The Prose Edda*, 93.
5. Sturluson, "The Ynglinga Saga," in the *The Heimskringla Saga,* Laing, trans., verse 4.
6. Sturluson, "Havamal," in *The Poetic Edda*, Crawford, trans., verse 140–41.
7. Bell, *Women of Classical Mythology*, 423.
8. Strabo, *The Geography of Strabo*, 205.

9. Sturluson, *Edda*, Faulkes, trans., 2–3.
10. Morgan, "History of Britain from the Flood to A.D. 700," 14.
11. Derolez, *Runica Manuscripta*, xv.
12. Sigurdsson, "Snorri's Edda: The Sky Described in Mythological Terms," 187.
13. Vigfusson and Powell, trans., *Corpus Poeticum Boreale*, 29.
14. Vigfusson and Powell, trans., *Corpus Poeticum Boreale*, 143.
15. Hollander, *The Poetic Edda*, 202.
16. Davidson, *Astronomy & the Imagination*, 130–34.
17. Vigfusson and Powell, trans., *Corpus Poeticum Boreal*, 94.
18. Crawford, *Poetic Edda*, 44.
19. Vigfusson and Powell, trans., "Old Play of the Wolsungs," in *Corpus Boreale Poeticum*, 30.
20. Vigfusson and Powell, trans., "The Sibyl's Poet: Volo-spa—The Sibyl's Prophecy," in *Corpus Poeticum Boreale*, 198–99.
21. Saxo Gammaticus, in Vigfusson and Powell, trans., *Corpus Poeticum Boreale*, 423.
22. Antonsen, *Runes and Germanic Linguistics*.

THREE FAMILIES OF RUNES

1. Derolez, *Runica Manuscripta*, xviii.

1. FEHU: CATTLE OR WEALTH

1. "Cotton MS, Domitian A–9, Saec XI," in Derolez, *Runica Manuscripta*, 7.
2. Vigfusson and Powell, trans., *Corpus Poeticum Boreale*, 23ff.
3. Vigfusson and Powell, trans., *Corpus Poeticum Boreale*, 69ff.
4. Bellow, trans., *The Poetic Edda*.
5. Vigfusson and Powell, trans., *Corpus Poeticum Boreale*, 92ff.

2. URUZ: WILD BULL OR UR: WATER

1. Caesar, *De Bello Gallico*, 28.
2. White, trans., *The Book of Beasts*, 219.
3. Schimmel, *Mystery of Numbers*, 41–42.

4. Caesar, *The Conquest of Gaul*, 146.
5. Boutsikas, "Knowing When to Consult the Oracle at Delphi."
6. Derolez, *Rúnica Manuscripta: The English Tradition*, 8.
7. Colless, "The Origin of the Alphabet."
8. Elliott, *Runes: An Introduction*, 19.
9. Vigfusson and Powell, trans., "Havamal," in *Corpus Poeticum Boreale*, 26.
10. Rohde, *The Old English Herbals*, 18.
11. Smythe, "Learn the History of the Nine Herbs Charm."
12. Vigfusson and Powell, trans., *Corpus Poeticum Boreale*, 422.
13. Sturluson, *Edda*, Anthony Faulkes, trans., 30, 87.
14. Vigfusson and Powell, trans., *Corpus Poeticum Boreale*, 422.
15. Dutton, *From the Mouth of Odinn: A New Translation of "Havamal,"* verse 13.
16. Ellis-Davidson, "The Ring on the Sword."

3. THURS: GIANT OR THORN

1. Thorsson, *Runelore*, 189.
2. "Sigrfdrifumal," Vigfusson and Powell, trans., in *Corpus Poeticum Boreale*, 42.
3. Vigfusson and Powell, trans., *Corpus Poeticum Boreale*, 427–30.
4. Davidson, *Scandinavian Mythology*, 78.
5. Barowski, "Mars, the Roman God of War."
6. Allen, *Star Names*, 308.
7. Strurlson, *Heimskringla: History of the Kings of Norway*, 6.
8. Crawford, trans., *Poetic Edda*, 65.
9. Vigfusson and Powell, trans., "Grimnismal," in *Corpus Poeticum Boreale*.
10. Sturluson, "The Ynglinga Saga," in *The Heimskringla Saga*. Verse 6.
11. "Havamal," Crawford, trans., 44.
12. Dashu, "Herbs, Knots, and Contraception."

4. ANSUS: HIGH GOD OR OSS: MOUTH

1. Adams, *Encyclopedia of Indo-European Culture*, 330.
2. Crawford, trans., *Poetic Edda*, 44.
3. Pennick, *Runic Lore & Legend*, 89.

4. Bellows, trans, *The Poetic Edda*, 89.
5. Vigfusson and Powell, trans., "Sigrfridumal," in *Corpus Poeticum Boreale*, 41.

5. RAIDO: JOURNEY

1. Crawford, "Havamal," in *The Poetic Edda*, 45.
2. Rees and Rees, *Celtic Heritage, Ancient Tradition in Ireland and Wales*, 191.
3. Vigfusson and Powell, trans., "Sigdrifumal," in *Corpus Poeticum Boreale*, 42.
4. Vigfusson and Powell, trans., *Corpus Poeticum Boreale*, 430.
5. Green, *Calendar of Festivals*, 61.
6. Derolez, *Runica Manuscripta: The English Tradition*, 7.
7. Sturluson, "Skaldskaparmal," in *Edda*, 155.
8. Herodotus, *The History of Herodotus*, Rawlinson trans., 208.
9. Davidson, *Scandinavian Mythology*, 67.
10. Sturluson, "Skaldskaparmal," in *The Prose Edda*, Brodeur, trans., 154.
11. Vigfusson and Powell, trans., "Grimnismal," in *Corpus Poeticum Boreale*, 70–71.

6. KEN: TORCH OR KAUN: ULCER

1. Sturluson, "Skaldskaparmal," in *Edda*, Faulkes, trans., 67.
2. Sturluson, "Prologue," in *The Prose Edda*," Brodeur, trans., 9.

7. GYFU: GIFT

1. Vigfusson and Powell, trans., "Grimnismal," in *Corpus Poeticum Boreale*, 75.
2. Herodotus, *The History of Herodotus* IV, Rawlinson, trans., 230.
3. Pennick, *Celtic Sacred Landscapes*, 49.
4. Vigfusson and Powell, trans., "Saxo Grammaticus," in *Corpus Poeticum Boreale*, 423.
5. Gudbrand and Powell, trans., "Sigrdrifumal," in *Corpus Poeticum Boreale*, 40.
6. Vigfusson and Powell, trans., "Sigrdrifumal," in *Corpus Poeticum Boreale*, 41.
7. Crawford, trans., *The Poetic Edda*, 45.

8. "The Names of the Days of the Week - Origin and Meaning," *The Names of the Weekdays*, The Viking Ship Museum website.
9. Malmstrom, *Cycles of the Sun, Mysteries of the Moon*, 204–207.
10. Bell, *Women of Classical Mythology*, 164.
11. Larrington, trans., "Voluspa," in *The Poetic Edda*, 11.
12. Thomson, *Studies in Ancient Greek Society*, 293.

8. WUNJO: JOY

1. Vigfusson and Powell, trans., "Groa's Chant," in *Corpus Poeticum Boreale*, 95.
2. Vigfusson and Powell, trans., "Sigrfridumal," in *Corpus Poeticum Boreale*, 43.
3. Davidson, *Myths and Symbols in Pagan Europe*, 16.
4. Ellis, *Dictionary of Celtic Mythology*, 215.
5. Morwyn, *Secrets of a Witch's Coven*, 215.
6. Sigfusson, *Havamal*, 27.
7. Grimal, *Dictionary of Classical Mythology*, 241.
8. Ellis, *A Dictionary of Irish Mythology*, 154.
9. Tolstoy, *The Quest for Merlin*, 209.
10. Derolez, *Runica Manuscripta*, 65.
11. Tolstoy, *The Quest for Merlin*, 145.
12. Page, *An Introduction to English Runes*, 82.

9. HAGALAZ: HAIL OR HEAL

1. Derolez, *Runica Manuscripta*, 10.
2. Vigfussen and Powell, trans., *Corpus Poeticum Boreale*, 94.
3. Fisher, *Labyrinth: Solving the Riddle of the Maze*, 144.
4. Vigfusson and Powell, trans., *Corpus Poeticum Boreale*, 43.
5. Rolle, *The World of the Scythians*, 27.
6. Davidson, *Astronomy and the Imagination*, 47.
7. Imperial Record Dept of India, *An Alphabetical List of the Feasts and Holidays of the Hindus and Muhammadans*, 45.
8. Campanelli, *Ancient Ways*, 36.
9. Larrington, trans., "Grimnismal," in *The Poetic Edda*, 11.
10. Davidson, *Roles of the Northern Goddess*, 155.

10. NAUDIZ: NEED

1. Sturluson, "Gylfaginning," in *Edda*, 26.
2. Grimm, *Teutonic Mythology*, Stallybrass, trans.
3. Dashu, "Seidstaffs of the Volur."
4. Sephton trans., *The Saga of Erik the Red*, Chapter 4, Verse 13.
5. Vigfusson and Powell, trans., "*Havamal*," 27.
6. Hollander, trans., "Voluspo," in *The Poetic Edda*, 9.
7. Vigfusson and Powell, trans., *Corpus Poeticum Boreale*, 184ff.
8. White, *Babylonian Star Lore*, 26.
9. Ions, *Indian Mythology*, 18.
10. Graves, *Greek Myths*, 126.
11. Vigfusson and Powell, trans., "Sigrdrifumal," in *Corpus Poeticum Boreale*, 41.
12. Larrington, trans., "Brynhild's Ride to Hell," in *The Poetic Edda*, 187.

11. ISAZ: ICE

1. Hershey, *Book of Diamonds*, 10.
2. Reynolds, "Regenerating Substances: Quartz as an Animistic Agent," 158–9.
3. Larrington, trans., "Havamal," in *The Poetic Edda*, 34.
4. Tacitus, *The Complete Works of Tacitus*, 731.
5. Heaney, trans., *Beowulf*, line 1290.
6. Homer, *The Iliad* Book 10, Robert Fagles, trans., line 300.
7. Brand, *Observations on the Popular Antiquities of Great Britain*, 315.
8. White, *The Book of Beasts*, 208.
9. Hymns and Carols of Christmas, "The Custom of Catherning."
10. White, trans., *Book of Beasts*, 225.
11. Krupp, *Beyond the Blue Horizon*, 150.
12. Rutherford, *Celtic Mythology: The Nature and Influence of Celtic Myth from Druidism to Arthurian Legend*, 117.

12. JERA: HARVEST OR PLENTY

1. Vigfusson and Powell, trans., *Corpus Poeticum Boreale*, 418.
2. Sturlson, "The Ynlinga Saga," in *The Heimskringla Saga*, Laing, trans., chapter 18.

3. Hand, *Horoscope Symbols*, 239.
4. Harrison, *Prologomena*, 146–50.
5. "The Ynglinga Saga," in *The Heimskringla*, Laing, trans., chapter 21–22.

13. IHWAZ: YEW TREE

1. Vigfusson and Powell, trans., *Corpus Poeticum Boreale*, 419.
2. Pliny the Elder, *Natural History*, Chapter 73.
3. Sturlason, "The Yngling Saga," in *Heimskringla*, Laing, trans., v 13–14.
4. Welle, "The Sky Disc of Nebra."
5. Ehser, Borg, and Pernicka, "Provenance of the Gold of the Early Bronze Age Nebra Sky Disk," 895–910.
6. Gyfaginning, *Edda,* Faulkes, trans., 55.

14. PERTH: DICE BOX

1. Bellows, trans., *The Poetic Edda*, 5.
2. De Santillana and von Dechend, *Hamlet's Mill*, 419.
3. Budge, *From Fetish to God*, 42.

15. ALGIZ: ELK OR ELK SEDGE

1. Oxford English Dictionary, "elk: Etymology."
2. Opie and Opie, *The Lore and Language of Schoolchildren*, 148.
3. Davidson, *Astronomy and the Imagination*, 130–34.
4. Tacitus, *The Complete Works of Tacitus*, 714.
5. Sturlurson, *Edda*, Faulkes, trans., 14.

16. SOWILO: SUN

1. Derolez, *Runica Manuscripta*, 7.
2. Damas, *Mythic Ireland*, 100.
3. Rohde, *The Old English Herbals*, 38–9.
4. Campbell, "Viking 'Sunstone' May Have Existed, Claim Scientists."
5. Vigfusson and Powell, trans., "Sigrdrifumal," in *Corpus Poeticum Boreale*, 28.

6. Larrington, trans., *The Poetic Edda*, 35.
7. Crawford, *Saga of Ragnar Lodbrok*, xxv.
8. Schimmel, *Mystery of Numbers*, 216.

17. TIUWAZ: GUIDING STAR

1. Psalm 119:131.
2. Manjo, *Healing Hand*, 88–89.
3. Lichtheim, *Ancient Egyptian Literature,* vol 2, 120.
4. Schimmel, *Mystery of Numbers*, 219.
5. "Meaning of Numbers in the Bible: The Number 17," Bible Study website.
6. Vigfusson and Powell, trans., *Corpus Poeticum Boreale*, 28.
7. Walker, *The Woman's Dictionary of Symbols and Sacred Objects*, 516.
8. Larrington, trans., "Voluspa," in *The Poetic Edda*, verse 55.

18. BERKAN: BIRCH OR POPLAR

1. Derolez, *Runica Manuscripta*, 10.
2. "Cortex - Etymology, Origin & Meaning," *Etymonline.*
3. Elliott, *Runes: An Introduction*, 65.
4. Gutsell and Johnson, "Wildfire and Tree Population Processes," (abstract).

19. EHWAZ: HORSE

1. Seleem, *Illustrated Egyptian Book of the Dead*, chap. 100.
2. Worm, *Runir seu Danica Literatura Antiquissima*, 102–3.
3. Etheridge, "A Systematic Re-Evaluation of the Sources of Old Norse Astronomy," 4.
4. Sturluson, *Edda*, Faulkes trans., 14.
5. Sturluson, "Skaldskaparmal," in *Edda,* Faulkes, trans., 93.

21. LAGUZ: LAKE

1. Evans, *An Introductory Dictionary of Lacanian Psychoanalysis*, 145.
2. Klingenberg, "Die Runeninschrift aus Bülach," in *Helvetia Archaeologica* 7, 116–21.

3. Crawford, trans., *The Saga of the Volsungs*, xn1.
4. McGrath, "Mimir and Volsi: What Were Those Herbs?"
5. Brodeur, trans., "Skaldskaparmal," in *The Prose Edda*, 144.

22. INGWAZ: EARTH GOD

1. Grammaticus, *The Nine Books of the Danish History of Saxo Grammaticus*, Book V, 157.
2. Bray, trans., *The Elder or Poetic Edda: Commonly Known as Sæmund's Edda*, 101.
3. Vigfusson and Powell, trans., "Long Lay of Brunhild," *Corpus Poeticum Boreale*, 293.
4. Davidson, *Gods and Myths of the Viking Age*, 104.
5. Harding, "Origin of the Harding Name and the Hardinger."
6. Grammaticus, *The Nine Books of the Danish History of Saxo Grammaticus*.
7. Grammaticus, *History of the Danes*, 12.
8. Davidson, *Gods and Myths of the Viking Age*, 143.

24. OTHALA: HOMELAND OR INHERITANCE

1. Revelations 22:23.

Bibliography

Adams, Douglas Q. *Encyclopedia of Indo-European Culture.* Taylor & Francis, 1997.

Allen, Richard. *Star Names.* Dover Publications, 1963.

Antonsen, Elmer H. *Runes and Germanic Linguistics.* De Gruyter, 2011.

Apollonius. *Voyage of the Argo.* Translated by E. V. Rieu. Penguin, 1987.

Ashe, Geoffrey. *Mythology of the British Isles.* Methuen, 1993.

Aswynn, Freya. *Leaves of Yggdrasil.* Woodbury, Llewellyn, 1990.

Atwood, M. A. *Hermetic Philosophy.* Julian Press, 1960.

Barnes, Michael P. *Runes.* Boydell Press. 2012.

Barowski, Janelle. "Mars, the Roman God of War: Overview & Facts." Study. Com, Accessed 11/21/2023.

Bayley. Harold. *Hidden Symbols of the Rosicrucians.* Sure Fire Press, 1988.

———. *Lost Language of Symbolism.* Lanham, MD: Rowman & Littlefield, 1968.

Bell, Robert. *Women of Classical Mythology.* Oxford University Press, 1991.

Bellows, Henry Adams. *The Poetic Edda.* Translated from the Icelandic with an Introduction and Notes by Henry Adams Bellows. The American-Scandinavian Foundation, 1923.

Benfey, Theodore. *Sanskrit-English Dictionary.* Asian Educational Services, 1991.

Bible Study. "Meaning of Numbers in the Bible: The Number 17." Biblestudy.org. Accessed 30 May 2025.

Boutsikas, Efrosyni. "Knowing When to Consult the Oracle at Delphi." Acadamia website, 2005.

Brand, John and Henry Ellis. *Observations on the Popular Antiquities of Great Britain: Chiefly Illustrating the Origin of Our Vulgar Customs, Ceremonies, and Superstition*. Henry G. Bohn, 1849.

Bray, Olive, trans. *The Elder or Poetic Edda: Commonly Known as Sæmund's Edda*. Viking Club, 1908.

Brodeur, Arthur Gilchrist. "Introduction to the Prose Edda." In *The Prose Edda*. American-Scandinavian Foundation, 1916.

Brodeur, A.G. trans. "Skaldskaparmal." Internet Sacred Text Archive (website), 1916.

Budge, E. A. Wallis. *From Fetish to God*. Dover Publications, 1988.

———. *Egyptian Language*. Dover Publications, 1983.

———. *Egyptian Magic*. Dover Publications, 1971.

Caesar, Julius. *The Conquest of Gaul*, bk. 6, chap. 28. Translated by S. A. Handford. Penguin Books, 1982.

———. *De Bello Gallico*, vol. 6. Bloomsbury Academic, 1982.

Campanelli, Pauline. *Ancient Ways*. Llewellyn, 1992.

Campbell, Charlie. "Viking 'Sunstone' May Have Existed, Claim Scientists." Time website, March 11, 2013.

Carmichael, Alexander. *Carmina Gadelica*. Lindesfarne, 1992.

———. *Carmina Gadelica*. Internet Sacred Texts Archive (website), 1900.

Clark, R. T. Rundle. *Myth and Symbol in Ancient Egypt*. Thames & Hudson, 1978.

Colless, B.E. "The Origin of the Alphabet." Academia website, 2014.

Crawford, Jackson, trans. *The Poetic Edda*. Hackett Publishing, 2015.

———. *The Saga of the Volsungs: With the Saga of Ragnar Lothbrok*. Hackett Publishing, 2017.

Damas, Michael. *Mythic Ireland*. Thames & Hudson, 1991.

Dashu, Max. "Herbs, Knots, and Contraception." 2004. Acadamia website

Dashu, Max. "Seidstaffs of the Volur." Suppressedhistories.net. Accessed June 13, 2025.

Davidson, H. R. Ellis. *Gods and Myths of the Viking Age*. Barnes & Noble, 1996.

———. "The Ring on the Sword," *Journal of the Arms and Armour Society*, 2 (1958).

———. *Scandinavian Mythology*. Peter Bedrick Books, 1988.

———. *Myths & Symbols in Pagan Europe*. Syracuse University Press, 1988.

———. *Roles of the Northern Goddess*. Routledge, 1998.

Davidson, Norman. *Astronomy and the Imagination: A New Approach to Man's Experience of the Stars*. Routledge, 1985.

Derolez, Réne. *Runica Manuscripta: The English Tradition*. Ghent University, Faculty of Arts and Philosophy, 1954.

De Santillana, Giorgio, and Hertha von Dechend. *Hamlet's Mill*. David R. Godine, 1992.

Dickins, Bruce. *Runic and Heroic Poems of the Old Teutonic Peoples*. Cambridge University Press Reprints, 2017.

Dillon, Judith. *The Alphabet and the Mystery Traditions*. Inner Traditions, 2024.

Diringer, David. *The Alphabet: A Key to History of Mankind*. Philosophical Library, 1948.

———. *Writing*. Praeger Publishers, 1967.

Du Fu. *The Poetry of Du Fu*, vol. 2. Edited by Stephen Owen et al. Translated by Stephen Owen. De Gruyter, 2016.

Dutton, Douglas. *From the Mouth of Óðinn: A New Translation of Hávamál*. Academia website.

Ehser, Anja, Gregor Borg, and Ernst Pernicka, "Provenance of the Gold of the Early Bronze Age Nebra Sky Disk." *European Journal of Mineralogy* 23, no. 6 (2011): 895–910.

Elliott, Ralph W. V. *Runes: An Introduction*. St. Martin's Press, 1989.

Ellis, Peter. *Dictionary of Irish Mythology*. Oxford University Press, 1987.

———. *Dictionary of Celtic Mythology*. Oxford University Press, 1992.

Etheridge, Christian. "A Systematic Re-evaluation of the Sources of Old Norse Astronomy." *Culture and Cosmos* vol. 16, no. 1 and 2. (Oct. 2012): 119–130. Academia website.

Evans, Dylan. *An Introductory Dictionary of Lacanian Psychoanalysis*. Routledge, 1996.

Fisher, Adrian. *Labyrinth: Solving the Riddle of the Maze*. Harmony Books, 1990.

Gikatilla, Joseph. *Gates of Light*. Translated by Avi Weinstein. HarperCollins, 1994.

Gimbutas, Marija. *Goddesses and Gods of Old Europe*. University of California Press, 1982.

———. *Language of the Goddess*. Harper & Row, 1989.

———. *Civilization of the Goddess*. HarperCollins, 1991.

Grammaticus, Saxo. *History of the Danes*. Translated by Peter Fisher. Boydell & Brewer, 1996.

———. *The Nine Books of the Danish History of Saxo Grammaticus*, translated by Oliver Elton. Norroena Society, 1905, Project Gutenberg website.

Graves, Robert. *The White Goddess*. Farrar, Straus, and Giroux, 1966.

———. *Greek Myths*. Pelican Books, 1982.

Green, Miranda. *Symbol & Image in Celtic Religious Art*. Routledge, 1992.

Green, Marian. *Calendar of Festivals*. Element Books, 1991.

Grimal, Pierre. *Dictionary of Classical Mythology*. Blackwell Publishing, 1986.

Grimm, Jacob. *Teutonic Mythology*. Translated by James Steven Stallybrass. George Bell and Sons, 1882

Gutsell, Sheri L., and Edward A. Johnson. "Wildfire and Tree Population Processes." *Plant Disturbance Ecology* (2007): 441–485. Science Direct website.

Haeffner, Mark. *The Dictionary of Alchemy*. The Aquarian Press, 1991.

Hand, Robert. *Horoscope Symbols*. Schiffer Publishing, 1981.

Harding, Steve. "Origin of the Harding Name and the Hardinger." University of Nottingham website.

Harrison, Jane. *Prologomena*. Princeton University Press, 1991.

Heaney, Seamus, trans. *Beowulf*. Farrar, Straus, and Giroux, 2000.

Hershey, John Willard. *Book of Diamonds*. Hearthside Press, 1940.

Herodotus, *The History of Herodotus*, book 2. Translated by George Rawlinson. Tudor Publishing, 1947.

Hollander, Lee, trans. *The Poetic Edda*. University of Texas Press, 1962.

Homer. *The Iliad*. Translated by Robert Fagles. Viking, 1990.

Hymns and Carols of Christmas. "The Custom of Catherning." The Hymns and Carols of Christmas website. Accessed 23 May 2025.

Ions, Veronica. *Indian Mythology*. Hamlyn, 1973.

Imperial Record Department of India. *An Alphabetical List of the Feasts and Holidays of the Hindus and Muhammadans*. Superintendent of Government Printing, 1914.

Jean, Georges. *Writing The Story of Alphabets and Scripts*. Abrams Books, 1992.

Jensen, Hans. *Sign, Symbol & Script*. Putnam, 1969.

Kaplan, Aryeh, trans. *The Bahir*. Weiser Books, 1990.

———. *Sefir Yetzerah: The Book of Creation*. Weiser Books, 1997.

Kelly, Edward. *Theatre of Terrestrial Astronomy*. Kessinger Publishing, 1988.

Kieran, Barry. *Greek Qabalah*. Weiser Books, 1999.

Klingenberg, H. "Die Runeninschrift aus Bülach." In *Helvetia Archaeologica*, 7 (1976): 116–21.

Koller, Aaron. "The Alphabet: The First Thousand Years." *Ancient Near East Today* (2020). Academia website.

Krupp, E. C. *Beyond the Blue Horizon: Myths and Legends of the Sun, Moon, Stars, and Planets*. HarperCollins, 1991.

Larrington, Carolyne, trans. *The Poetic Edda*. Oxford University Press, 2014.

Lichtheim, Miriam. *Ancient Egyptian Literature*, vol 2. University of California Press, 1976.

Lurker, Manfred. *Gods and Symbols of Ancient Egypt*. Thames & Hudson, 1984.

Malmstrom, Vincent H. *Cycles of the Sun, Mysteries of the Moon*. U. of Texas Press, 1997.

Manco, Jean. *Ancestral Journeys*. Thames & Hudson, 2013.

Manjo, Guido. *The Healing Hand: Man and Wound in the Ancient World*. Harvard University Press, 1975.

Matthews, John. *The Celtic Reader: Selections from Celtic Legend, Scholarship and Story*. Aquarian, 1991.

McGrath, Sheena. "Mimir and Volsi: What Were Those Herbs?" *We Are Star Stuff: A Blog About Mythology*. Earthandstarryheavens.com. March 24, 2019.

Millar, Angel. "The Old English Rune Poem—Semantics, Structure, and Symmetry." *Journal of Indo-European Studies* 34, nos. 3 and 4 (Fall/Winter 2006).

Morgan, R.W. Hist*ory of Britain from the Flood to A.D. 700: Compiled from the Various Ancient Records*. Marshall Press, 1933.

Morwyn. *Secrets of a Witch's Coven*. Schiffer Publishing, 1988

Napier, David. *Masks, Transformation and Paradox*. University of California Press, 1986.

Nonnus. *Nonnos Dionysiaca with an English Translation by W.H.D. Rouse. Mythological Introduction and Notes by H.J. Rose; and Notes on Text Criticism by L.R. Lind 2*, Books 16–35. Edited by T.E. Page et al. Translated by W.H.D. Rouse. Harvard University Press, 1956.

Novo Scriptorium. "Archaeological Evidence from Bulgaria Shows That Ancient Thrace Was Part of the Cretan-Mycenaean Culture." Novoscriptorium.com, January 6, 2020.

Online Etymology Dictionary. "Cortex - Etymology, Origin & Meaning." Etymonline.com. Accessed 30 May 2025.

Opie, Iona, and Peter Opie. *The Lore and Language of Schoolchildren*. Oxford University Press, 1959.

Oxford Classical Dictionary, 2nd ed. Oxford University Press, 1972.

Oxford English Dictionary, "elk: Etymology," Oed.com.

Page, R. I. An Introduction to English Runes, 2nd ed. Boydell, 1999.

Parker, Eleanor. *Winters in the World: A Journey through the Anglo-Saxon Year*. Reaktion Books, 2022.

Pennick, Nigel. *Celtic Sacred Landscapes*. Thames & Hudson, 1996.

———. *Runic Lore & Legend*. Destiny Books, 2019.

Pliny the Elder. *Natural History Book VIII: The Nature of the Terrestrial Animals*. Edited by John Bostock and H.T. Riley. Taylor and Francis, 1855. Perseus Digital Library, Tufts University website.

Poe, Richard. *Black Spark, White Fire*. Prima Publishing, 1999.

Potter, Samuel. *A Compend of Materia Medica, Therapeutics, and Prescription Writing*. P. Blakiston Son & Company, 1917.

Price, Neil. *A History of the Vikings*. Basic Books, 2020.

Pritchard, James, ed. *Ancient Near East*. Princeton University Press, 1958.

Reader's Digest. *Magic and Medicine of Plants*. Reader's Digest Association, 1986.

Rees, Alwyn, and Brinley Rees. *Celtic Heritage: Ancient Tradition in Ireland and Wales*. Grove Press, 1961.

Reynolds, Ffion. "Regenerating Substances: Quartz as an Animistic Agent." In *Time and Mind: The Journal of Archaeology, Consciousness and Culture*, vol. 2, issue 2 (July 2009): 153–166.

Rohde, Eleanour Sinclair. *The Old English Herbals*. Longmans, Green and Co., 1922.

Rolle, Renate. *The World of the Scythians*. University of California Press, 1980.

Rutherford, Ward. *Celtic Mythology: The Nature and Influence of Celtic Myth from Druidism to Arthurian Legend*. Weiser Books, 1990.

Sanders, Seth. *The Invention of Hebrew*. University of Illinois Press, 2009.

Sephton, J., trans. *The Saga of Erik the Red: A Translation*. D. Marples and Co. Limited, Melvill Chambers, 1880. Project Gutenberg website, 2016.

Schimmel, Annemarie. *The Mystery of Numbers*. Oxford University Press, 1993.

Scholem, Gershom. *Origins of the Kabbalah*. Translated by Allan Arkush. Princeton University Press, 1990.

Schwartz, Howard. *Tree of Souls: The Mythology of Judaism*. Oxford University Press, 2004.

———. *On the Kabbalah and Its Symbolism*. Schocken Books, 1996.

Seleem, Ramses. *Illustrated Egyptian Book of the Dead*. Sterling Publishing, 2001.

Serviss, Garrett. *Astronomy with the Naked Eye*. Harper & Brothers, 1908.

Shaw, Miranda. *Passionate Enlightenment*. Princeton University Press, 1995.

Sigurdsson, Gisli. "Snori's Edda: The Sky Described in Mythological Terms." In *Nordic Mythologies: Interpretations, Intersections and Institutions*. Edited by Timothy R. Tangherlini. North Pinehurst Press, 2014.

Skelton, Robin, and Margaret Blackwood. *Earth Air, Fire, Water: Pre-Christian and Pagan Elements in British Songs, Rhymes and Ballads*. Arkana Publishing, 1990.

Smoley, Richard. *Forbidden Faith: The Secret History of Gnosticism*. Harper, 2006.

Smythe, Lynn. "Learn the History of the Nine Herbs Charm." The Creative Cottage website, 2020.

Spalinger, Anthony. "Epagomenal Days in Ancient Egypt." *Journal of Near Eastern Studies*, 54 (January 1995).

Strabo. *The Geography of Strabo*, vol. 7. Edited by T.E. Page et al. Translated by H.L. Jones. Harvard University Press, 1960.

Strassfield, Michael. *Jewish Holidays*. Harper Row, 1985.

Sturluson, Snorri. *The Prose Edda: Tales from Norse Mythology*. Translated by Jean Young. University of California, 1954.

———. *The Prose Edda*. Translated by Arthur Gilchrist Brodeur. American-Scandinavian Foundation, 1916.

———. *Edda*. Translated by Anthony Faulkes. Everyman's Library, 1995.

———. *The Heimskringla Saga: Or the Chronicle of the Kings of Norway*. Translated by Samuel Laing. E. P. Dutton, 1961. Internet Sacred Texts Archive website, Accessed May 19, 2025.

———. *Heimskringla: History of the Kings of Norway*. Translated by Erling Monsen and A. H. Smith. Dover Publications, 1990

Tacitus, Cornelius. *The Complete Works of Tacitus*. Edited by Moses Hadas. Translated by Alfred John Church and William Jackson Brodribb. Random House, 1942.

Tangherlini, Timothy. *Nordic Mythologies: Interpretations, Intersections and Institutions*. North Pinehurst Press, 2014.

Thompson, George. *Studies in Ancient Greek Society*. Citadel Press, 1965.

Thorsson, Edred. *Runelore*. Weiser Books, 1988.

Titchenell, Elsa-Brita. *Masks of Odin*. Theosophical University Press, 1985.

Tolstoy, Nikolai. *The Quest for Merlin*. Little Brown and Company, 1985.

Trungpa, Chogyam, and Francesca Fremantle. *Tibetan Book of the Dead*. Shambhala, 1987.

Vigfusson, Gulbrand, and F. York Powell, trans. *Corpus Poeticum Boreale: The Poetry of the Old Northern Tongue from the Earliest Times to the Thirteenth Century*, vol. 2. Clarendon Press, 1883.

Walker, Barbara. *The Secrets of the Tarot*. Harper Row, 1984.

———. *The Woman's Dictionary of Symbols and Sacred Objects*. Harper Row, 1988.

Waal, Willemjin."Mother or Sister? Rethinking the Origins of the Greek Alphabet and Its Relation to the Other 'Western' Alphabets." In *Understanding Relations Between Scripts II: Early Alphabets*. Edited by Philip Boyes and Philippa Steele. Oxbow Books, 1950.

Welle, Deutche. "The Sky Disc of Nebra." Biblioteca Pleyades website, 2002.

Walters, Derek. *Chinese Geomancy*. Element Books, 1989.

———. *The Alternate I-Ching*. Aquarian Press, 1987.

West, John Anthony. *Serpent in the Sky*. Quest Books, 1993.

Wethered, H. N. *The Mind of the Ancient World: A Consideration of Pliny's Natural History*. Longmans, Green and Co., 1937.

White Gavin. *Babylonian Star Lore*. Solaria Publications, 2014.

White, Lynn. *Medieval Technology*. Oxford University Press, 1962.

White, T. H., trans. *The Book of Beasts: Being a Translation from the Latin Bestiary of the Twelfth Century*. Putnam, 1954.

Wolkstein, Diane, and Samuel Noah Kramer. *Inanna: Queen of Heaven and Earth; Her Stories and Hymns from Sumer*. Harper & Row, 1983.

Wong, Eva. *Cultivating the Stillness*. Shambhala, 1992.

Worm, Ole. *Runir seu Danica Literatura Antiquissima* [Runes: The Oldest Danish Literature]. Martzan & G. Holst, 1651.

Zori, David. *Age of Wolf and Wind: Voyages through the Viking World*. Oxford University Press, 2024.

Index